"Just Trust Us"

"Just Trust Us"

The Erosion of Accountability in Canada

By

J. Patrick Boyer

BREAKOUT EDUCATIONAL NETWORK
IN ASSOCIATION WITH
DUNDURN PRESS
TORONTO · OXFORD

Publisher: Inta D. Erwin
Editor: Amanda Stewart, First Folio Resource Group
Designer: Bruna Brunelli, Brunelli Designs
Printer: Webcom

National Library of Canada Cataloguing in Publication Data

Boyer, J. Patrick
    Just trust us: the erosion of accountability in Canada/by J. Patrick Boyer.

One of the 16 vols. and 14 hours of video which make up the
    underground royal commission report
Includes bibliographical references and index.
ISBN 1-55002-431-0

    1. Responsibility—Canada. 2. Political corruption—Canada.
3. Canada—Politics and government—1984–1993. 4. Canada—Politics
and government—1993–. 5. Representative government and
representation—Canada. I. Title. II. Title: underground royal
commission report.

JL65 B69 2002   352.3'5'0971   C2002-902311-4

1   2   3   4   5   07   06   05   04   03

Care has been taken to trace the ownership of copyright material used in this book. The author and the publisher welcome any information enabling them to rectify any references or credit in subsequent editions.
                                                          J. Kirk Howard, President, The Dundurn Group

Printed and bound in Canada.
Printed on recycled paper. ♻
www.dundurn.com

Cover Photo Credits:
MacKenzie King: National Archives of Canada
St. Laurent: Canadian Consulate General
Diefenbaker: National Film Board
Pearson: Canadian Consulate General
Trudeau: Canadian Embassy
Clark: Canadian Heritage Gallery
Turner: Canadian Consulate General
Mulroney: Progressive Conservative Party of Canada
Campbell: Progressive Conservative Party of Canada
Chrétien: Canadian Heritage Gallery

Exclusive Canadian broadcast rights for the *underground royal commission* report

intelligent television

Check your cable or satellite listings for telecast times

Visit the *urc* Web site link at:
www.ichanneltv.com

About the *underground royal commission* Report

Since September 11, 2001, there has been an uneasy dialogue among Canadians as we ponder our position in the world, especially vis à vis the United States. Critically and painfully, we are re-examining ourselves and our government. We are even questioning our nation's ability to retain its sovereignty.

The questions we are asking ourselves are not new. Over the last 30 years, and especially in the dreadful period of the early 1990s, leading up to the Quebec referendum of 1995, inquiries and Royal commissions, one after another, studied the state of the country. What *is* new is that eight years ago, a group of citizens looked at this parade of inquiries and commissions and said, "These don't deal with the real issues." They wondered how it was possible for a nation that was so promising and prosperous in the early 60s to end up so confused, divided, and troubled. And they decided that what was needed was a different kind of investigation — driven from the grassroots 'bottom,' and not from the top. Almost as a provocation, this group of people, most of whom were affiliated with the award winning documentary-maker, Stornoway Productions, decided to do it themselves — and so was born the *underground royal commission*!

What began as a television documentary soon evolved into much more. Seven young, novice researchers, hired right out of university, along with a television crew and producer, conducted interviews with people in government, business, the military and in all walks of life, across the country. What they discovered went beyond anything they had expected. The more they learned, the larger the implications grew. The project continued to evolve and has expanded to include a total of 23 researchers over the last several years. The results are the 14 hours of video and 16 books that make up the first interim report of the *underground royal commission*.

So what *are* the issues? The report of the *underground royal commission* clearly shows us that regardless of region, level of government, or political party, we are operating under a wasteful system ubiquitously lacking in accountability. An ever-weakening connection between the electors and the elected means that we are slowly and irrevocably losing our right to know our government. The researchers' experiences demonstrate that it is almost impossible for a member of the public, or in most cases, even for a member of Parliament, to actually trace how our tax dollars are spent. Most disturbing is the fact that our young people have been stuck with a crippling IOU that has effectively hamstrung their future. No wonder, then, that Canada is not poised for reaching its potential in the 21st century.

The *underground royal commission* report, prepared in large part by and for the youth of Canada, provides the hard evidence of the problems you and I may long have suspected. Some of that evidence makes it clear that, as ordinary Canadians, we are every bit as culpable as our politicians — for our failure to demand accountability, for our easy acceptance of government subsidies and services established without proper funding in place, and for the disservice we have done to our young people through the debt we have so blithely passed on to them. But the real purpose of the *underground royal commission* is to ensure that we better understand how government processes work and what role we play in them. Public policy issues must be understandable and accessible to the public if they are ever to be truly addressed and resolved. The *underground royal commission* intends to continue pointing the way for bringing about constructive change in Canada.

— Stornoway Productions

14 hours of videos also available with the *underground royal commission* report.
Visit Stornoway Productions at www.stornoway.com for a list of titles

This book is dedicated to
Joan Andrew,
a steadfast friend and loyal Canadian patriot

Acknowledgments

I am indebted to Kitson Vincent, an erudite and independent Canadian whose ideas and friendship have inspired me in the creation of this book. Inta Janovskis Erwin has worked tirelessly and creatively to translate into reality the dream of an educational network that can help us break out from the institutional and intellectual prison of stale practices; this book is but one small expression of that larger effort. Alexandra Chapple has likewise brought youthful energy and intelligent freshness to our mission, and I am grateful that she and I see the world in the same colours. Paul Kemp has matured and evolved from his early days as a researcher with the *underground royal commission* into a skilled writer and editor, intelligent producer and independent thinker. He has been a reliable consultant on the story in this book. Juliette Cooper has, with determined focus, helped carry this small text through its numerous revisions. Editors Amanda Stewart and Fran Cohen have used every known device and skill to shape the manuscript into its present form. At the end of the seesaw struggles over what should go, what should stay, and the nature of current word usage and punctuation, I salute their accomplishments and am thankful for their painstaking professionalism. Kirk Howard, president of The Dundurn Group, friend and resilient Canadian publisher, has continued to be astute and clear, and as enterprising as ever.

To Douglas Fisher — dean of the Parliamentary Press Gallery, wise and sanguine student of the passing political parade, mentor to many of us who deeply care about making parliamentary government a functioning reality in contemporary Canada, and friend for 35 years — I am truly grateful, both for the honesty of his foreword to this book, in which he does not flinch from the truth, and for his steady encouragement to me over the years, which helped me write this book in the first place. Douglas was for eight years a member of Parliament, but he is a lifelong parliamentarian.

Joan Andrew has been like an adoptive mother over the years since my beloved wife, Corrine, died in 1995. She has kept order in my household and humour in my life, and her supportive insistence in helping to maintain the isolated existence that a writer's life requires has proven to be as inventive as it has been welcome. Since she made possible the completion of many earlier and longer versions of this book, she more than richly deserves having this one, which finally made it through the press, dedicated to her.

Alison McQueen, in a class by herself among the many energetic and highly intelligent students it has been my privilege to teach at the University of Toronto, Wilfrid Laurier University and the University of Guelph in the years since I left public life, has inspired me in the completion of this book, and provided fresh eyes. When the student is ready, the teacher will appear. Each of us is a student. As she herself would note, quoting Marcel Proust, "The real voyage of discovery consists not in seeking new landscapes, but in having new eyes."

Finally, to all those who supported me in my decade in public life, I express enduring gratitude. It is a humbling honour to be an elected representative of the people in Canada's national Parliament. Their efforts and encouragement sent me into the battles of the arena, where I acquired an ever greater passion for the aspirations we Canadians share. That is the energy driving the story I now tell, in the hope that we can break free from all that is holding us back.

Table of Contents

Who We Are

Where We Are Going

Foreword

My friendship with Patrick Boyer began in Ottawa during Canada's centennial year, when he and I would occasionally run into one another on Parliament Hill and chat about the state of the nation and its political affairs. Patrick was 21 then and not yet through law school; he had recently spent some time travelling across the country querying young Canadians about their ideas and prospects. I was settling into a fresh career as a newspaper columnist and TV commentator based in the Parliamentary Press Gallery, after eight years as an NDP MP (1957–65).

In his determination to understand the political system and how it worked, Patrick was more precocious than most young people I had met who were intent on politics — for example, Brian Mulroney and Joe Clark. Even then, Patrick was thinking about the fairness and effectiveness of the system more than political parties or participation. What we found in common — as I saw it — was a mutual interest in parliamentary reform. In retrospect, having read *"Just Trust Us"* and learned more about Patrick's perspective, I belatedly appreciate that the critical framework of his interest and subsequent study was far more encompassing, and also more legal and philosophical, than mine. Even from 1984 to 1993, when he was a remarkably busy Tory MP, he always kept "the whole" at the forefront of his critical thinking, rather than becoming consumed by the course or fate of a particular party or his own career.

I came to Parliament excited by what I would be able to do to further my key interests (like forestry, transport and Aboriginal affairs), but within a year of my first speech in the House of Commons I was restive. Lord knows it was not from lack of opportunities to speak in the House or draft reports in committees; nor did it stem from the relative lack of influence I had or the lack of attention my concerns were given. What was most frustrating to me was that the services and resources I had at hand were inadequate for me to be a truly effective MP. I also quickly came to dislike the often adolescent partisan rivalry that permeates parliamentary activity in this country. No active MP could escape this partisanship (and regretfully I was often a willing and accomplished practitioner of it). Eventually I decided to voice my concerns in Parliament. So one night in the House, early in the second Diefenbaker mandate, I rose and asked that MPs be better paid. Along with more pay I wanted a qualified clerical person full time and access to printing services and research assistance. My request elicited a storm of disapproval from Victoria to Bonavista, even from the elders in my own party. This negative reaction only deepened when I circulated petitions supporting the provision of paid travel tickets and long-distance calls to and from one's constituency. After some months, and with the strong backing of Speaker Roland Michener, Cabinet grudgingly approved my "reforms." These initiatives began my career as a parliamentary reformer, a role I have kept at for over 40 years — seeking, for example, more time and attention for bills and motions put forth by back-bench MPs; more independence from the party whips; more responsibility for parliamentary committees; and freer access to data from government departments and Crown corporations. Of course I was not alone in this, though I estimate that less than one in 10 MPs have ever regularly pushed for change in or reform of Parliament, say, like the late Ged Baldwin or Gordon Fairweather did — or as Patrick Boyer did when he was a member in the House, or as he is doing now by authoring this book.

I now see clearly that my approach and that of so many others was incremental, bit by bit. Looking back at Parliament over the past four decades, one finds an intermittent string of various reforms or changes implemented to make MPs more useful and Parliament more capable in its ability to make laws and scrutinize spending. Because of reforms, for example, parliamentary committees on occasion have the opportunity to analyze and suggest amendments to very complex bills after first reading, and they have the power to hold hearings across Canada and travel outside the country; the Speaker of the House is now selected by MPs through a secret ballot rather than by the prime minister; the number of reference specialists in the Library of Parliament has increased, from two in 1957 to more than 70 by 1990; and departmental spending estimates are now dealt with by specialized committees rather than by the whole House. (In *"Just Trust Us"* Patrick Boyer singles out this last "reform" as a particularly unwise move that has rendered the examination of government spending a farce.)

In recent years I have come to accept that despite such "improvements," or in some cases because of them, the importance of the House of Commons and the roles played by MPs has been weakened; indeed, even the role of Cabinet ministers has been diminished as the media and the public increasingly turn their attention only to the prime minister and his office. Not long ago I found myself speculating on something quite repugnant: that the present system can only be rescued and returned to vigorous plain dealing and accountability by the arrival of a "saviour" of sorts — a new prime minister dedicated to reducing the enormous power of his or her own office. In doing so, I was conceding that in all my years of pursuing changes I had focused on the individual MP and his or her activities without fully comprehending the huge shift that was taking place in government, right before my eyes — a shift to a more highly disciplined partisanship, tied to a cult of leadership and very tight party control of parliamentary work.

In *"Just Trust Us"* Patrick Boyer introduces his readers to this wider, loftier perspective. He examines both the interplay of all orders of government — federal, provincial, municipal and megacity — and the ceaseless connections we all have with their laws, regulations and services. This work has taken him above rather than away from Parliament Hill. His lucid, grim analysis of what he sees as a fundamental change in the Canadian character satirically exposes the recently developed cliché of the "Canadian way" — that kinder, gentler, more responsible way — for what it truly is: a convenient way to rationalize why we have developed from a self-sufficient, financially and socially responsible country into a society that looks to government to meet virtually all of its needs and wants.

Boyer demonstrates that as the "Canadian way" evolved into being, the institutional "tripwires," alarms that warn us of mistakes or misgovernment, were abandoned. Parliament has lost its substance and become hollow. Ministerial responsibility is a sham. The so-called public and private sectors have melded into one, knit together by the countless interest groups, associations and lobbyists that populate a country with more government and government employees per capita than any other in the Western world. The end result is that our government today operates like a sponge, soaking up almost all of us through our condition and requirements as citizens. In fact, we have become so fully absorbed by this Great Canadian Sponge that we can no longer clearly separate ourselves from it. We remain blissfully unaware of or tacitly accept without outrage the waste, overlap, inefficiency, boondoggling and nepotism that are rampant within our government, and the attendant diminution of both the capability of and opportunities for our elected representatives to influence legislation and closely check government performance and spending. The result, Boyer concludes, is that "there really is little or no accountability in Canadian government today, despite the formal appearance of it." I can vouch for the truth of that opinion.

The discourse in *"Just Trust Us"* will ring true for the skeptical citizen, and it will no doubt provide a reality check for those who continue to extol the Canadian way as "the best" or even as "very good." This is not a tract for a political party but an analysis of a national condition that *can* be corrected once its reality and causes are widely known. My generation, in its prime in World War II, and several subsequent ones created the problems we have today; the solution will likely come from the energy and idealism of those who are now in their teens, 20s and 30s. Yet if they are to succeed, they must not lose sight of this crucial truth: before we can undo the mistakes of the past, we have to clearly understand how and why the mistakes were made in the first place, and how the system as it exists today came to be.

Douglas M. Fisher
July 2002

Introduction

This book seeks to understand the erosion of accountability that we experience in Canadian government today in terms of the processes, decisions and institutional changes that got us here.

Rather than providing an academic or facile solution — a "Top 10" checklist of enhancing measures to ensure good government — this work is founded on the belief that the most important and effective changes emerge from an in-depth understanding; an understanding to which these chapters, I hope, can contribute.

The material here is intended not so much to lead to action — although ideally that will follow — but rather to cause reflection, to stimulate rethinking of democratic accountability from a citizen's perspective.

The kind of accountability called for in this book is not of the blame-game variety, the sort that drives officials from public office or provides the juice for sensational scandal. Aggressive accountability already has plenty of breathless practitioners. Here we use accountability instead as a higher observation deck from which to see — and perhaps see clearly for the first time — what is really happening, or not happening, across

Canada's political landscape, with a fresh perspective and from a somewhat detached vantage point. Climbing to the top of a tower or being aloft in an airplane can often give us a sudden comprehension of relationships and positions that had previously escaped our notice because they simply could not be seen from the ground. Being aloft does not mean being aloof. It may mean being able to connect the dots, to make sense of our surroundings and understand our anger, frustration and confusion by seeing with new eyes the context that necessarily has generated those inexplicable yet very real feelings in the first place.

Gaining this somewhat detached perspective in order to benefit from a clear and dispassionate view of our present circumstances has been greatly aided by the remarkable work of something called the *underground royal commission*. Eight years ago a group of citizens started its own inquiry into our country's affairs. At first it seemed like a good idea for a major television documentary (many members of the group had worked previously with the documentary filmmaker Stornoway Productions). As they delved further into their research, these citizens increasingly sensed that the *official* royal commissions and public inquiries established by governments to deal with specific issues or policies were not touching, deeply or comprehensively, the real challenges facing Canadians.

So they decided to turn their television documentary into something much larger: a comprehensive investigation of Canadian governance that would survey the thoughts, feelings and opinions of Canadian citizens with diverse backgrounds and experiences. The 23 researchers who travelled across Canada conducted over 400 interviews and compiled more than 600 hours of video footage. It wasn't just who was being interviewed that mattered; it was, equally, who was asking the questions. As Plato taught long ago, getting the question right is the most important step toward discovery.

I have used the insights gleaned from these interviews to develop and support the arguments presented in this book, and blended them with what I have learned from my own experiences — as a member of Parliament, as a university professor of political science, and as someone who has participated actively, for as long as I can remember, in our country's political and public policy organizations. Readers may encounter some things they do not believe, some assertions that may seem to emerge from unwarranted cynicism. Yet these observations are the end product of an extensive research and interview process meant not to be rampantly critical, but to seek genuine understanding. Where I have quoted specific individuals in the pages that follow, unless otherwise noted, their comments are excerpts from interviews with researchers from the *underground royal commission*; more extensive transcripts of these interviews can be found in many of the other 15 books that resulted from this research.

Although this book, like the work of the *underground royal commission* itself, is all about stepping out of the problem as much as possible in order to truly see it, it is not written with disinterest. If I did not care with profound passion about Canada, you would not be holding this book right now. The important point to remember is that in order to fix any difficult or complex problem, we first have to come to a clear understanding of what the problem is and how it was created. It is only once we've gained this understanding that we can then focus our attention on finding effective and lasting solutions.

Patrick Boyer
September 2002

What Has Happened

1. The Citizen's Perspective in a Democratic Country

When I left public office in 1993 after a decade in Parliament, the single deepest concern I took with me was the vast gap between the theory of Canadian government and its actual practice. What we teach the children in civics courses is not the way it really is.

What we teach children, of course, is that Canada has "responsible government," meaning that our government is *responsible to the elected representatives of the people*. We explain that in practice this means the executive officials who run the government (the prime minister and Cabinet ministers), being themselves elected members of the House of Commons, are required to explain to Parliament what they are doing with their power in the course of governing the country.

Usually we do not bother to add that this can be a hassle. Most people like to be left alone to get on with doing their jobs, busy Cabinet members included, without being bombarded by incessant "Whys?" like the parent of a young child. Moreover, most of the questions asked by parliamentarians are partisan and are just intended to inflict political damage, while the hard-hitting questions asked around Parliament Hill by pesky journalists typically seek to expose scandals and contradictions and yield explanations the government ministers would prefer not to give. Given this prickly and explosive atmosphere, not to mention the urgent need to get on with the important work of governing when there's so little time available, it is understandable that most of the time an embattled and busy prime minister or Cabinet minister would just as happily bypass the House of Commons on his or her way to the office.

Despite this human instinct to avoid the unpleasantness of face-to-face interrogation, hostility and ridicule — which is only exacerbated by the confrontational way our House of Commons is constructed, like a battle pit for adversaries — the reality is that this is what passes for "accountability" in our system of government. Ministers cannot escape being held accountable because our Constitution requires that those who wield political power answer and give account in Parliament to the citizens' elected representatives. That's what "responsible government" means.

We also teach kids that responsible government means the government (as represented by Cabinet) must have the "confidence" of a majority of other elected representatives in the House of Commons. This confidence, so-called, is more than a state of mind; it is measured by votes. It means that to stay in office and run the country, the Cabinet ministers must consistently achieve and maintain the voting support of a majority of the members of Parliament. If a government measure is defeated in a parliamentary vote because fewer MPs vote for the proposed bill or resolution than against it, the government itself, as sponsor of the legislation or motion, is also deemed defeated and must leave office. It is at this point in the parliamentary drama that we citizens are then called on to rethink who should govern, as a new general election must be held to replace the fallen government. In our history this has happened several times.

There are a few wrinkles, but that's essentially how, since back to the 1840s, even well before Confederation, it has worked in our country when it comes to who has the power of government and how they are held accountable to us for its use.

Generally, responsible government is not a hard sell because it just *sounds* so right. What more could we want or even expect from government than that it be responsible? The very idea of responsible government, enshrined in the Constitution, is deeply reassuring. Yet for most Canadians today there is a growing sense that although we may have responsible government in theory, in reality we have anything but. Ever since television cameras began to broadcast proceedings from the House of Commons, exposing the general public more and more to what *really* goes in Parliament, a deep and accelerating alienation from government has been under way across Canada. People at some point began to realize that responsible government had in many important respects become a farce.

TV did not itself directly cause this change. Sure, "telepolitics" has transformed public affairs and election campaigns into entertainment, and the visual drama on our screens has in some ways become a substitute or proxy for the personal participation that once gave political parties and governing institutions greater salience in our lives. TV did not cause the change so much as it reported on the effects of the deeper story being told in this book, namely, how our venerable institutions and practices meant to achieve accountability first atrophied into irrelevance, then descended into irresponsibility. Indeed, our entertainment-saturated society paid little attention to this development precisely because it was so unspectacular; slow meltdown is less dramatic than a single explosion, and it's hard to get high viewer ratings in our fast-paced clicks-per-second age by showcasing the "drama" of the hard-to-visualize and ever-so-gradual demise of our political institutions and value systems. Thus the process was mostly untelevised and largely unrecognized. Yet the result has been the same: Canadian government is no longer responsible. In the past year I have even heard people use the word "embarrassing" to describe the way Ottawa now runs the show.

Another reason this development was hard to see is that getting perspective is not easy. Perspective requires distance, the kind we need to notice things clearly. A clear and dispassionate view of our present circumstances — to the extent that humans can ever achieve this — helps delineate who we are, what our institutions do and why our conditions have become what they are. We often get so busy with the tumble of urgent daily affairs that we lack the greater distance needed to see historical perspectives and gain balanced insights about the relative significance of what's coming at us on the pulsating TV screen, or what the prime minister said today, or especially what we suspect isn't even being reported at all.

Perhaps, above everything, the reason it has been hard for us to notice this decrease in accountability is that most of what we know about government is presented from the government's own institutional and self-protecting perspective, rather than from the citizen's point of view.

We once used that word, "citizen," to speak about individuals in relation to government. Today, however, this term is seldom heard. Government officials and their advisors busy themselves in lofty ways with concepts and processes that tend to leave out real live, breathing, smelling, feeling, energetic and emotional people. The common folk, so to speak. Under such conditions, those who hold high positions in public office become increasingly manipulative of the citizenry (and, necessarily, their elected representatives) instead of responsible to them. This is exactly what has happened in Canada, where today most actions and programs are evaluated in terms of their consequences for government rather than their impact on the Canadian people. I remember spotting a newspaper headline that read "Breakthrough on Housing for Canada's Poor," but when I keenly put my coins in the box and extracted a copy, I discovered, as I stood there in the street reading the news, that the "story" was not about how Canada's ill-housed were going to get a better deal, but merely how federal and provincial government officials had renegotiated inter-jurisdictional responsibilities for existing public housing programs. This was not an isolated experience. The phrase "government of the people, by the people, for the people" still rolls off many tongues in moments of rhetorical flourish, but in truth our system can be more accurately described as "government of the government, by the government, for the government." Officials and policy consultants no longer talk about people as "citizens"; we have become "clients" and "customers" and "stakeholders," and are spoken of as "demographics" and "targets."

Today, at beginning of the 21st century, Canada is confronting serious problems, many of which are of a different order from those we have faced in the past. Our government is heavily indebted, uncertain about security, ambiguous in public goals and faced with constitutional doubt. Our country is hobbled by a strongly entrenched separatist movement in Quebec; the prosperity gaps between Atlantic and central Canada that existed *before* 30 years of "regional economic expansion" have yet to be closed; and a deep sense of "apartness" continues to disconnect Western Canada from the rest of the country.

Beyond all this, endemic and intractable as such smouldering crises may appear, lurk other problems of a different nature. Voter turnout in

Canadian general elections has been in steady decline in recent years, a hugely significant development. According to Elections Canada, in 1988, 75.3 percent of eligible voters cast ballots; in 1993, turnout had fallen to 69.6 percent; by 1997 it was 67 percent, and by 2000, 61.2 percent. This falling away by citizens is also measured by the growth of the underground economy and the rising levels of tax avoidance and tax evasion. This reluctance of citizens to participate in the governing system, whether expressed by declining to vote or by refusing to pay taxes, is evidence of a deeper shift, an indication that Canadians are turning away from and have become alienated by our governing institutions. Judges tell me an increasing number of witnesses seem to have no fear of perjuring themselves in the witness box. As a university professor, I am newly mindful of the ease with which plagiarism now occurs in the age of the Internet. There is a growing gap between older institutions and the behaviours they require for successful operation, and current practices. This phenomenon is reinforced by opinion surveys which suggest that something serious has changed in the beliefs, values and attitudes of Canadians. The proportion of Canadians who feel "government doesn't care what people think" rose from 45 percent in 1968 to 67 percent in 1993. Confidence in the House of Commons fell from 49 percent in 1974 to 21 percent in 1996. The proportion expressing "a great deal" of confidence in political parties fell from 30 percent in 1979 to 11 percent in 1999. In 2000 the Canadian Elections Survey found that a total of 24.8 percent, or one in four Canadians, was "not very satisfied" or "not at all satisfied" with the way democracy works in Canada.

Evidently something needs fixing. Yet what? At the university where I now teach, colleague Richard Phidd, a professor of public administration and public policy, observed how "beneath the surface of all the proposed organizational changes we contemplate, and certainly beneath the surface of those reforms being actually implemented, are conflicting and competing norms, values and ideas which operate in the direction opposite to such reforms."[1] The *context* in which decisions are made and changes occur is therefore of the highest significance.

So before taking any remedial action, it's important to get a better grasp of our situation. How easy is that? A citizen today faces the daunting reality that the problem of Canada may itself be too large to be seen, too complex for individual skills. Even well-educated, well-off and well-connected Canadians who seem to master their own situations pretty well and who can see the interplay between cause and effect in their personal lives encounter this problem when it comes to the government of the country. Individuals daily consider pros and cons and decide between spending money on this year's foreign vacation or sending a daughter through one more year of university, between putting time and energy into an added room at the cottage or taking a night course to qualify for a promotion, or between spending extra time with an ailing dad or playing golf with the business buddies. Personally we show that we understand not only choice, but also the concept of "opportunity cost" that goes with it: if we choose to do one thing, it will consume time, energy and money in ways that preclude doing another thing instead.

Yet when it comes to evaluating decisions of government, to moving our thinking up to the bigger picture, these linkages and tradeoffs evaporate. Worse, the pros and cons, the causes and their effects, often can't even be brought to mind for evaluation. There is no ready form, forum or procedure, no way for an individual citizen to truly connect with or evaluate our government, which means, in turn, that we cannot appreciate the consequences of the demands we make upon our government. What comes next? When government is amorphous, incomprehensible and disconnected, we do not even need to weigh choices and tradeoffs; we just make claims and demands without worrying about the potential costs because we vaguely sense that someone else will somehow pick them up. Or, if we do consider costs, we tend to become almost self-righteous in expressing a view that "the system" owes us such a benefit, given all the taxes we're paying and how little we're getting back!

So what is an individual to do? The traditional replies — go to meetings, sign a petition, join a political party, participate, vote, write a letter to the editor — don't cut it anymore for the simple reason that such activities don't connect to anything real. The citizens who have begun to boycott our elections are perhaps merely holding up a mirror to show the rest of us how dysfunctional the system in which we're still play-acting has really become. Over the past 30 years or so, including the decade when I myself was a member of Parliament, I have encountered many citizens who repeatedly sought to take civic action only to be overpowered by a political-governmental-bureaucratic juggernaut. A sinking feeling set in when they realized "doing something" meant going head to head against bureaucracies, political parties, old boys' networks, cultural establishments, journalistic attitudes, special-interest organizations and lobby groups.

I saw many Canadians who felt they had no place to turn. A large number grew cynical and passive. The falling away from politics and the decline in voter turnout are not quirks; they are a direct consequence of the growing feeling of powerlessness within the Canadian public. Ironically, as a member of the House of Commons I experienced a similar reaction. Even though I no doubt appeared to my constituents to be more of a political-system insider than they were, in Ottawa I often found myself like some hapless mountain climber trying to scale the sheer face of an immense plate-glass window. It was fitting, I thought, that an entire constituency of citizens would send to Ottawa as their stand-in and spokesperson someone who would confront the same feelings of powerlessness and ineffectiveness they did. Perhaps this is what it really means when we say we have *representative* democracy!

What becomes clear, from this and other evidence, is that a key element in our theory of responsible government is not being carried out and, dishearteningly, perhaps is not even capable of being carried out, in practice. This is the role of holding government accountable. The concept of "accountability" means being bound to give an account; it means being responsible *for* things and being responsible *to* someone else. Accountability is how we figure out, as best we can, what happened. It is how we connect causes with effects, partly to correct mistakes and to do better next time. Accountability is the process through which those who govern are held responsible for their decisions by the governed.

We live by trial and error. This means we try things and make mistakes. It is not said that we live by "trial and success" for the simple reason that we do not learn nearly so much from our successes — when everyone is happy, feeling a bit smug and taking a satisfied measure of credit — as we do from a screw-up, when instead we have to sort through the wreckage to figure out what went wrong. The reason we want to keep on living and doing things is not because the whole world — and each of us in it — is perfect or that we know only success. It is because we have flaws and actually like to rise to the challenge of figuring out what they are and fixing them. Canadians have earned a respected reputation for our many clever inventions, as we prove time and again to be adept at improvising in the face of limited resources or arranging things in new ways to solve puzzling problems. As in life, so in government. Our system of accountability through responsible government, for years thought to be one of our cleverest inventions of an institutional kind, was mandated by our Constitution, tacitly embracing the long-understood truth that failure is the salt of life.

Yet no Canadian government or public office holder is politically motivated to show mistakes; instead they are pressured to cover them up or put a "spin" on otherwise damaging information. This government-perspective instinct to avoid the reporting of mistakes means, in turn, that important lessons are not being learned. Or at best they are only being learned after all the political and administrative hurdles that self-protecting governments defensively erect around themselves have been heroically cleared away.

Accountability, accordingly, should be thought of as much more than a blame game. It is more than aggressive cynicism represented by a "gotcha" style of journalism, more too than the premeditated posturing for partisan advantage before the television cameras in Question Period. Across the country accountability is exercised daily in each of our lives. When it comes to politics and government, why should the same bite of realism not be present? In organized human society there is a reasonable expectation that we should seek to apply our resources to meet our needs, and that we should do so with at least some correlation between cost and benefit, some thought to initial purpose and ultimate result. Just because we cannot forecast the future does not mean we should be inattentive to our present circumstances, be unmindful of past mistakes and lessons from history, or fail to look at what those who exercise control over us are doing with their power. Indeed, not to insist upon political accountability in this higher and more profound sense today amounts to being irresponsible about tomorrow.

Understood in this context, accountability does not imply narrow or judgmental faultfinding. In talking about government and Parliament, we can quickly scoot past the blame game once we realize there's always more than enough blame for everyone to have a share. The system as it is currently functioning is more than adequately focused on that sharp form of accountability — putting individuals on trial in the court of public opinion, and occasionally in the law courts as well.

Accountability in the broader sense, however, means recognizing and accepting that political actions and government decisions have consequences. It means knowing what those consequences are and understanding the need to evaluate them in terms of costs and benefits. It means, especially, understanding that making choices is much more than a function of either partisan politics or market forces; ultimately choices are a matter of ethics, character and culture.

The important point is to take note of what we're actually doing. What if, in our real world, we have grown so confused about government that we no longer know where reality ends and illusion begins? If we don't know this, how can we ever hope to have accountability in government? In reality the only standard left us by which to check government performance would be our state of confusion. In such an airtight trap it would not be abnormal for government to just keep going in circles. It would in fact be natural — which may be why the mindlessly repetitive patterns in Canadian government also seem so recognizable and familiar to us, even when they don't make sense. "Just one more in a series of reports telling us what we should do," exclaimed an exasperated June Callwood over CBC airwaves in early May 2002, as yet another government study on child poverty in Canada was released. Meanwhile, over the past decade the number of Canadian children living in poverty increased: from one child in seven living below the poverty line to one in five.

Inevitably, the more confusing government becomes and the more counterproductive it appears, the more a sane person will disconnect, tune out. Consider, for example, the confusion that arises from the government's penchant for initiating royal commissions. A royal commission is an extensive study that typically entails hiring a platoon of researchers. The result is a report that usually comes out years later, but by then the underlying issue that gave rise to the inquiry in the first place has invariably been transformed by the passage of time and intervening events. This may not be bad from the government's point of view. Delay is often the hidden hope of the government that initiates the royal commission. It is, from the perspective of those comfortable in power and seeking to look like leaders while maintaining the status quo, a highly rational device to buy time and diffuse potential crises, our well-tested Canadian recipe for extended procrastination.

These elaborate studies of big issues, in theory intended to develop a comprehensive view of a problem and come up with recommendations, represent a particularly Canadian way of *appearing* to provide good government while in fact escaping accountability. Indeed, the royal commission is the perfect example of how government itself generally operates in Canada. It is institutional. It is extensive. It is expensive. It is unaffected by the rising of the tides or the changing of the seasons. The overall outcome is only haphazardly connected to the stated original purpose, and the results are seldom acted upon. While at first blush it appears setting up a royal commission would be the ultimate responsible act by government, Canadian political history reveals it to be, instead, one of the most elegant escape mechanisms from accountability we have yet devised.

Government by royal commission represents an alternative form of policy formation and decision making that lies well outside the constitutional structures of parliamentary government and democratic political accountability. Not only does government by royal commission largely bypass Parliament, but it also serves to hollow out Parliament in the process. Each time one is instituted, another major area of public policy is removed from the operational agenda of responsible government. This practice of commission government has been going on for so long in Canada now that the attitudes and behaviours which it engenders have themselves contributed to the demise of Parliament as a relevant institution in national government. If you ask members of Parliament themselves, many would even say that Parliament is not able to deal with the big and complex issues that form the mandates of royal commissions and judicial commissions of inquiry. It's as if those elected to represent us like the political game, but as ringside spectators who don't want to play for real in the big leagues.

So what happened next? Although many Canadians turned off and tuned out, not everyone did. It was precisely the expensive failures and the fragmented approaches to Canada's innumerable problems, as exemplified by the reports from Canada's endless parade of royal commissions, not to mention the often ineffective policy results flowing from the advice of senior civil servants and influential lobbyists, that provoked a group of concerned Canadian citizens to take action in what came to be a self-styled *underground royal commission*. They wanted to examine public policy from a citizen-centred rather than government-centred perspective, to look for accountability and evaluate the effectiveness of responsible government for themselves.

I first became aware of Canada's *underground royal commission* and its team of researchers in late autumn of 1993. They contacted me, I was told, for a variety of reasons: my prior work as a journalist in Ontario, Saskatchewan and Quebec; my experience working as a lawyer across Canada as a partner in a major Toronto law firm; and my experience in national political life, including a decade "in the engine room" of Parliament and a stint as parliamentary secretary at both External Affairs and National Defence. The *underground royal commission* thought that with this background I could help evaluate some of its findings and contact people I knew as further leads for investigation.

My involvement with this organization brought me into contact with individuals from such diverse fields as journalism, theatre, television, government, business and non-governmental organizations, as well as educators, farmers, people in the resource economy and social workers. Rather than speaking much with established political pundits or Canadian media commentators (who tend to bathe in the same intellectual bath water anyway), the *underground royal commission* researchers sought out the opinions of the country's saltier "experts" — cattle ranchers in the West; sawmill operators in New Brunswick; investment dealers and manufacturers in Ontario; wheat farmers on the Prairies; East Coast fish plant operators; Alberta oilmen; economists, historians and legal authorities in Quebec; as well as professors, candid citizens and government officials who work (or have worked) behind the scenes in municipalities, provincial capitals and along the banks of the Rideau River.

The lens through which the *underground royal commission* chose to examine Canadian government focused squarely on accountability. Once we begin to look at Canadian government through such a lens, we see connections that link the things we've been troubled about but that have not previously been explained in terms of the shortcomings of our system of responsible government. Important questions then start to emerge. For example, does large-scale tax avoidance or a huge underground economy just start spontaneously one morning? Do Prairie farmers simply get up on the wrong side of the bed one day and start protesting the marketing constraints of the Canadian Wheat Board? How do businesspeople calling for freedom from government regulation end up in the queue asking for government subsidies? If Parliament is accountable for controlling public spending, how did we manage, under its watchful eye, to achieve a national debt that still stands at $540 billion as of this year?

The researchers wanted to get at the root cause of the problems we Canadians are facing by dissecting the actual nature and accountability practices of real government programs. We can read textbooks on how responsible government *should* work, but the *underground royal commission* also wanted to understand how contemporary Canadian government *actually* functions. The researchers would try to gain a citizen's perspective in a democratic country. Accordingly, their investigations began, not at our country's head office in Ottawa, but closer to home, those authentic places where citizens earn and learn daily, where the reality of government hits the streets. What they discovered is that the problems we are facing in Canada did not just happen spontaneously. They developed over time and had specific causes. Very real explanations exist for why the public mind soured, why consent among the governed withered away, why government lost its corrective controls and why Parliament abdicated its primary role of calling to account those who wield power.

This book, along with the video documentaries and 15 other publications in this series, together form what might be called the "first interim report" of the *underground royal commission*. The conclusions of this report have tended to confirm, but also to expand upon, what I observed during my years as an MP in Ottawa: there is little or no accountability in Canadian government today, despite the formal appearance of it. Moreover, many of Canada's problems — from our multibillion-dollar national debt to regional economic inequalities, from the rise of separatism to the unusual perils facing our Armed Forces, from crippling levels of taxation to voter apathy — can all be traced back to this absence of accountability.

In the following chapters I'll present some evidence gathered by the *underground royal commission* and share lessons I've learned from my experience as an MP to help show how, in the actual day-to-day operations of government, we have strayed surprisingly far from the concept of responsible government once envisioned by the Fathers of Confederation, and still formally outlined in our Constitution.

2. The Case of the Missing Tripwires

As humans we survive, and can even prosper, because of built-in sur-vival mechanisms. We are guided by basic senses like sight, hearing and touch working through the brain's powerful system for processing information. These senses are supplemented by our intuition or "sixth sense," a characteristic further enriched by wisdom and seasoned through experience. These all then combine to co-ordinate our physical responses.

We also surround ourselves with mechanical extensions of these survival mechanisms, things we've invented and built to protect us and make human society work. Electrical panels in our homes have fuses or breakers to cut an overheating circuit that could cause a fire. Factories are full of machinery that shuts down automatically when a critical dan-ger point is reached. Computers that run equipment have safety default positions. The launching of nuclear warheads is held in check (we des-perately hope) by a series of "fail-safe" systems.

Yet when it comes to our government, which we have also created, we have not been very successful in installing tripwires. In fact they often seem to be missing altogether. There is no reliable way to shut the system down when a demonstrable mistake is occurring, or when there is a need for correction or repairs: the system just keeps operating. This phenomenon encapsulates, in matters of government, the absence of accountability. It is almost inexplicable. In many respects it now appears that we actually *refuse* accountability. Like a person whose behaviour is dangerous both to himself and others, we Canadians, as self-governing people, frequently behave in ways that are harmful to our own interests, even wilfully disobeying what we know we should do, as the chapters to come will demonstrate.

A still more haunting thought is this: what if we don't even *see* the danger signals? What if our system of government in Canada has come to consist of little more than self-reinforcing feedback loops?

It would be one thing if we operated under a primitive political system, one that had yet to evolve to the stage where we'd learned from mistakes and built into our governing institutions procedures to make them, if not fail-safe, at least broadly accountable. That's not us. We actually *had* such systems in place — the procedures and practices of responsible government — and got rid of them. Their strange absence from government today contributes to this distinct impression that we positively refuse to be accountable. Consider, for example, the following five checks or tripwires we once had:

Defined Jurisdictions for Government. Under the Constitution, only two jurisdictions are shared between the national and provincial governments: agriculture and immigration. Yet in practice *most* jurisdictions have been blurred; today it is hard to find any area in which there is not more than one level of government directly involved. This jurisdictional overlap has occurred, however, without the creation of any parallel institutional structure or mechanism for monitoring, evaluation and public accountability. The result is that constitutional accountability has gone missing in action.

Parliamentary Approval of Spending. At one time Parliament scrutinized all spending every year, department by department, line by line, proposed expenditure by proposed expenditure. Doing so took a long time. Yet it was the main business of Parliament because, for government, what you spend on shows what you support. Money is policy. The requirement to approve the spending estimates on a line-by-line basis was removed in 1969, when new legislation to "reform" Parliament was enacted, stating that departmental estimates would be automatically

36

deemed approved in June each year, even if Parliament hadn't looked at them. The result was that spending was no longer systematically reviewed by members of Parliament. Nor did civil servants fear, to the degree they formerly had, that it would be.

The Comptroller General. The original role of this official was to approve government spending, after it had been authorized by Parliament, only when he or she was satisfied that there was enough money to pay for it. The comptroller general provided pragmatic realism, for even if Parliament had authorized the spending levels requested in the Estimates, the government would not be able to spend money if in fact the cupboard was bare. The power of this effective control was eliminated in 1969. Thereafter government overspent, deficits ensued and the national debt rose.

Balanced Budgets. For decades Canada's ministers of finance viewed public revenue as money held in trust for the people. They only spent what they had (made easier in practice back then by the tight-fisted control of the comptroller general) and balanced the budget by matching revenues with expenses. If they had to go into debt to pay for extraordinary measures, such as winning a war, they resolutely paid down the money owed after the crisis had passed. This kind of thinking was replaced with Keynesian economics, which justified overspending in times of economic downturn. However, Keynes also advocated building a surplus in times of prosperity, a critical aspect of his theory that our government gradually chose to ignore. As a result, the Canadian government ran only deficits — no surpluses — for several decades, and the national debt rose.

Parliament in Balance with Government. Government has always dominated the Canadian political landscape. However, for an extended run government's role was counterbalanced by a more open parliamentary process. Certainly there are some measures a government must develop under the cloak of secrecy, but in a self-governing democracy with the accountability requirements of responsible government provided under our Constitution, occasions when such action is necessary are few. Yet government in Canada increasingly prevented open debate of policy directions and cut off strategic evaluation of alternative choices for the country. Parliament came to be treated as a ritual nuisance, an implementation device to ratify what the executive had already decided to do, rather than an integral part of the law-making process. Today

MPs lack, or fail to use, institutional means of control over government. As a result, far too many major government initiatives have failed to benefit from either course correction or public support, two crucial dimensions of accountability in a self-governing democracy.

How could these five established and fundamental tripwires, these mechanisms for accountability, be removed from our system of responsible government? In some cases those in power deliberately decided that the hot circuits of government should never blow a fuse (removing the effective controls on spending, for instance). In other cases checks and controls were diminished by a general drift that was not effectively resisted (such as blending together federal and provincial jurisdictions without simultaneously establishing any parallel monitoring mechanism).

We've noted how essential components of accountability have been removed, but what flowed next? Unaccountable government was certainly not operating in a void. Bureaucratic administration and the political imperatives of senior government officials required that procedures be followed; the result, over the course of several decades, was that unaccountable government became an established and familiar practice, surrounding our governing institutions with an aura of good governance despite accumulating evidence to the contrary.

3. Losing Constitutional Controls

How Absence of Accountability Became Institutionalized

What if, seen up close, our system of responsible government proves to be less a model of accountability than we taught ourselves to believe it was? Starting at the foundation is a good way to assess the strength and nature of Canada's edifice of government, which brings us to the familiar topic of our Constitution. By joining the principles of accountability and democracy, the Constitution of Canada outlines how, through the practices and norms of our self-governing society, we have the potential to hold those in office accountable for their exercise of power. That, as already noted in Chapter 1, is the essence of our system of responsible government. Now we are ready to examine just how strong this supporting foundation remains today.

Our leaders, because they face parliamentary scrutiny and general elections every few years, do encounter the potential for a reckoning. Yet what if a more specific examination of the workings of Canadian government showed a lack of effective scrutiny, or disclosed an inability to match stated goals with eventual outcomes? What if these trends became so rampant within the conduct of our public affairs as to constitute a virtual repudiation of responsible government? Failure of responsible government would mean an absence of accountability. Even worse, it could mean that lack of accountability had become institutionalized.

This is not easy to recognize. Locating any single point of accountability within the complex structures and convoluted operations of Canada's system of government may be challenging. It may even be impossible. When everyone is accountable, it turns out nobody really is; the buck, we discover the more we try to follow its circular path, stops nowhere. That's why Canadians can appreciate the story of four national delegates speaking on the subject of elephants. The British speaker entitles his address "The Empire and the Elephant." The American speaks on "How to Grow the World's Biggest and Best Elephants." The French orator warms his audience with an engaging presentation on "The Sex Life of the Elephant." The Canadian representative confronts this question: "The Elephant — A Federal or Provincial Responsibility?" Sure, that's us!

So how should we try to get a handle on the accountability of our institutions? In the big picture, two of the most important features of the Canadian Constitution are the doctrine of responsible government and the division of power between two levels of government. The first means the prime minister and Cabinet ministers (the executive of our country's government) must appear in the House of Commons to answer questions from members of Parliament about issues of the day. Ministers' explanations are a form of accountability, and as discussed earlier, this is what the term "responsible government" stands for in our parliamentary context. The second basic constitutional feature is what we call "federalism": the division of powers between two different governing jurisdictions (Ottawa and the provinces). This division of powers enables us to hold each level of government responsible for doing what it's supposed to do. Separated powers also help to guarantee citizens' freedom and protection from government simply because one level of government checks or balances the other. Thus, our Constitution provides for accountability in a two-fold fashion: through the existence of responsible government and by the allocation of functions in a structured manner.

The significance of the second of these mechanisms is clear from the brutal history of human society, which demonstrates that *power must be divided, not concentrated, and be accountable, not absolute.* The

20th century saw many horrific examples of self-aggrandizing power-mongers: Adolf Hitler in Nazi Germany, Josef Stalin in the Soviet Union, Pol Pot in Cambodia, Idi Amin in Uganda. The message here requires no decoding: human nature demands that power be diffused and restrained. Unaccountable power is a source of evil doings. Perhaps the greatest wisdom the Fathers of Confederation embedded in the Constitution is displayed in its division of power.

The federal form of political union means we have not one but two orders of government in the country, each sovereign within its own jurisdiction. At the same time, a federal union means there is a wide range of mutual interdependence, and that the actions of one government frequently affect the other. That is why a *working* federal system requires a great deal of co-operation between the two levels of government in order for citizens to have the economic, social and other policies that bring maximum benefits. Many formal and informal arrangements help to achieve such co-operation, but all the same, whenever spending, taxing or any other power is divided between two different governments, arguments and confrontations will inevitably arise.

The balanced allocation of powers outlined in the original constitutional design was always vulnerable, but during the second half of the 20th century it was lost entirely. This happened when the two levels, rather than working as independently as possible in their respective spheres of jurisdiction, began to interact, co-operate, intrude, grow together, overlap and duplicate; as the lines of jurisdictional responsibility became blurred, the threads of accountability became entangled and impossible to follow. Over this period we ended up with double government, and the resulting disharmony and ineffectiveness has since exacted a huge and needless price from us all. Determining how this balance was lost will help us understand how we lost accountability, despite the seemingly well-devised constitutional plan to divide jurisdictional powers.

Section 91 of the Constitution outlines Ottawa's general powers to provide for peace, order and good government. This section also enables the federal government to use taxation and expenditure to regulate the economy. It was never clear, however, how far the Government of Canada could go in using its taxing and spending power to regulate and affect activities that otherwise fell under provincial jurisdiction. Ottawa's rogue use of its power to spend has long been an issue (and has caused sparks to fly) in both Canadian courtrooms and legislative assemblies. Under Section 91(3), the Government of Canada may raise money by "any mode or system of taxation," a power that has resulted in direct taxes such as income tax, and indirect taxes such as customs and excise taxes. The direct ones we know we're paying because we see them. The indirect taxes are hidden because they are incorporated into the retail price of such products as liquor, gasoline and cigarettes. Provincial governments also have the power of taxation to fund activity in their areas of responsibility. Section 92 lists the kinds of things a provincial government can tax, for example, income taxes, property taxes, mineral, oil, natural gas and timber royalties, retail sales taxes, corporation taxes and death and succession duties. Any tax a province imposes must be direct, meaning it will be visible to taxpayers and not hidden from them the way some of Ottawa's taxes can be.

When it comes to what governments can do with the money they collect, Section 91 lists 31 categories in which the Government of Canada has exclusive authority to act. These range from trade and commerce, to military defence, to postal services, to shipping, navigation and weights and measures. However, this list *only illustrates but does not restrict* the power of the federal government. Ottawa can spend directly in *any field*. It can establish a Crown corporation to engage in any kind of business; there is no constitutional barrier. The rule of thumb is that whatever the Constitution does not address — what were innocently called "residual powers"— Ottawa gets. In this way, our federal system actually encourages governments to spend. If you have jurisdiction but don't occupy it with activity and programs (which obviously require spending money), the other level of government, being a rival power, will move in. Canadian political history demonstrates that this is precisely what happened, starting right after Confederation in 1867.

Such shifts in power, of course, did not happen suddenly, but evolved gradually as political pressures and judicial interpretations reshaped Canada's Constitution. A number of "doctrines" of constitutional interpretation developed over the decades following Confederation, with the courts seeking to give meaning to the Constitution's principles in changing contexts, as the country grew and conditions evolved. We have a dynamic, not a static, Constitution. Two doctrines that especially made it a "living document" were developed by the courts to encourage the federal and provincial authorities to work together through informal, ad-hoc constitutional adjustments. First, "even though it initially seemed to the courts that it was inconsistent with the intentions of the framers and the language of the text," as constitutional law professor David Beatty notes, the judges were able to work through a doctrine of "delegation," which effectively allows one level of government to ask the other to take charge of an area of public policy that would normally be its responsibility. Secondly, the Supreme Court upheld the constitutionality of Ottawa's "spending powers," whereby it makes grants of money (or taxes) available to the provinces for programs in health, education and welfare (areas primarily within provincial jurisdiction) on condition that these services are provided in a way that meets basic federal objectives.[2]

Once Ottawa began using this extraordinary power to spend in areas falling under provincial jurisdiction, it effectively began to override the Constitution. Obviously this advance by Ottawa through the intersection of powers should have been marked with a huge flashing red light, warning of legal challenges and political battles — or worse. For example, under the Constitution, provinces have jurisdictional control over their natural resources, but Ottawa moved into this area, asserting claims over provincial resources such as oil and natural gas. When the Trudeau government moved to take control of Alberta's resources with the National Energy Program, not only did the red light flash, but the alarm bell clanged through the long, cold night.

In addition to the memorable drama of the National Energy Program, over time the Canadian government took other major steps down this route into provincial jurisdiction, most notably by introducing shared-cost programs in which Ottawa provided "conditional grants" to the provinces. This money was given on the condition that the provinces abide by national laws setting out the terms under which the money could be used. In Ottawa's mind this was a responsible form of leadership that would establish national standards and ensure poorer provinces would not be bypassed as progress occurred elsewhere in the country. It was also consistent with the sense of nation building that had emerged among many Anglo-Canadians by mid-century. The federal government first introduced shared-cost programs for health insurance and highways, both being exclusively matters of provincial jurisdiction under the Constitution. In short order Ottawa was also using its power to pump money into other areas of provincial responsibility, such as municipal government, property housing and urban development and cultural programs such as the Canada Council. The Government of Canada, meanwhile, continued to act in areas of mutual jurisdiction with the provinces, where there already had been overlap of policy and confusion of effort. The result was that we Canadians were getting more government than we needed — in many fields and for many years.

All the while, provinces were likewise spending much more money in a wide range of areas, including social welfare, education, industrial development, environmental protection, highways, trade promotion, agriculture, resource development, telecommunications, hydroelectric power, consumer protection, health care, labour relations, law enforcement, municipal services and tourism. In the 1860s these were mostly minor jurisdictions, yet they proved to be sleepers, for by mid-20th century they had become giants in every respect. In the case of health and education, where sharp increases in costs meant that these areas began consuming most of the provincial budget, provinces often welcomed new spending by Ottawa. As a result, the lines of accountability, in jurisdictional terms, blurred further.

After World War II bold political leadership and new roles for government seemed to be the order of the day. Experience on the home front had shown Canadians how government could intervene in events with seemingly good results, and in the 1940s and 1950s Canada's political leaders spoke not of "national reconciliation" but of "national reconstruction." Some premiers even encouraged a dynamic and expanding role for Ottawa, and political energies and economic resources soon were parlayed into nation building across Canada, although certainly not in Quebec, as we shall see. The positive side of this new Canadian attitude emphasized growth and the creation of national standards. The negative dimension was that it failed to respect long-standing constitutional jurisdictions. The mood of the times and the actual needs across the land supported building the country. So that is what took place, accompanied by and also fuelling the post-war economic boom.

Time passed. Events unfolded according to this new national order. Meanwhile, in Quebec the fires of nationalism had been lit, fanned by a federal government intent on overriding provincial jurisdiction so it could spend money in the province. This flame smouldered deep in the hearts of the French-speaking people who, in a number of ways and by various powers and authorities, were being taken for granted, exploited and suppressed. This political fire continued to burn until, in the 1960s, it grew hot enough to ignite FLQ bombs.[3] Eventually other bombs of a political nature would start detonating across English-speaking Canada as well. This different series of explosions, however, would be triggered by the same phenomenon: a national government overspending in everyone's jurisdiction, overextending itself in the economy and creating a staggering national debt in the process. The political explosions began in the West, particularly Alberta.

This period after the war when such developments were occurring was a turning point in our history; the character of intergovernmental relations within the country underwent a profound change, and in the transformation we lost the constitutional fundamentals of political accountability. Our federal state had been irrevocably altered. Canada was no longer governed by a strong Constitution, but by a central government that made its own plans first, thought about provincial governments and jurisdictional limits second, and long-term financial viability third, if at all. Under the tax-rental agreements between Ottawa and the provinces, commenced during World War II, provinces qualified for payments from Ottawa based on a formula related to "tax points." At first Ottawa made payments and in exchange the provincial government temporarily yielded its taxing powers to consolidate tax collection and streamline government as part of the overriding war effort. After the war, though, the national government didn't give provincial taxing powers back; instead it renewed the tax-rental agreements and used the revenue to fund its new programs, such as unemployment insurance and medicare. Significantly, Quebec would not sign the 1947 and 1952 tax-rental agreements, although by 1957 it was again participating as a result of federal financial bullying tactics.

Tax-rental agreements altered the nature of intergovernmental relations and hence our prospects for accountability. For a fee, Ottawa would be the tax collector for a province. Since no government especially likes to collect taxes, this offer had, at least outside Quebec, certain appeal. By the same token, it's just as clear why Quebec was not interested in reshaping the character of the Canadian federal state: it is a major loss of control, indeed forfeiture of an element of sovereignty, to allow another government to bring in your money for you. Today Ottawa collects personal income taxes on behalf of all provinces except Quebec, and corporate income taxes on behalf of all provinces except Quebec, Ontario and

Alberta. The taxation agreement, set out under the Fiscal Arrangements Act, specifies how the provinces will be paid and the conditions they must meet. It's yet another arrangement that makes the provinces subservient to, and leaves them somewhat subsumed by, the federal government.

In 1967, moving even further down this road into provincial affairs — always, of course, in the "national interest" (as seen by Ottawa), the federal government introduced "equalization payments": unconditional payments made by rich provinces to poorer ones, administered through the agency of our national government. The goal was to spread Canada's wealth equally across the country. Who could possibly be against that? Although the goal was noble, application proved far from simple. Based on the abstract principle that every Canadian is entitled to a basic level of public services, equalization payments were meant to ensure that Canadians living in the poorer provinces would neither be forced to accept lower levels of services nor pay higher provincial taxes in order to receive such services. Yet putting this principle into practice was difficult because payments were calculated using a complex formula and changes in relative prosperity from time to time across the country meant altering the formula. For example, when Alberta and Saskatchewan became "have" provinces with huge oil and gas royalties, the formula changed. At one point even money-tree Ontario qualified for a transfer payment. Of course the rules were then hastily rewritten.

Over the decades these transfers made big differences in several ways. Some provinces came to depend on these payments. In Atlantic Canada transfer payments soon made up more than one-quarter of provincial government revenues. The effort to negotiate, renegotiate and administer this system developed into a major internal activity, as governments moved tax dollars around among themselves. The transfer-payment program reinforced the role Ottawa was increasingly taking, governing Canada as if it were a unitary (one government) state rather than a federation.

Shared-cost programs were another avenue through which federalism was revamped from the inside, even as formal or external appearances (as seen by the public) remained the same. As the federal government proceeded with new plans for "social engineering," shared-cost programs became its way of stimulating other levels of government to act — in those instances where Ottawa saw a need but believed it could not do anything directly on its own because of constitutional or other reasons. Shared-cost programs had major implications. They allowed the Government of Canada to introduce hospital insurance, medicare and the Canada Assistance Plan, paying half the costs of these programs to those provinces that agreed to participate. This money was a major incentive for many provincial governments. Yet by introducing hospital insurance and medicare programs on this shared-cost basis, the federal government pushed all the provinces into providing universal health care for Canadians on a plan that Ottawa thought best. Some provinces had already developed their own health-insurance programs, but Ottawa figured that, left on their own, the provinces would develop different standards. It calculated that the provinces could not afford to ignore the whopping incentive of national funding for fully half the cost: it is to spend dollars that only cost you 50¢. This type of conditional grant, in which one level of government was offering to pay only if certain conditions were met, forced participating provinces to comply with the national standards stipulated by Ottawa. Thus provinces like Ontario and Manitoba, which already had in place their own effective hospital-insurance programs on a well-funded basis, were forced to revamp their programs or else miss out on money that other provinces were scooping up.

Understandably, most provinces resented these shared-cost programs. They felt that the Government of Canada, not content just to govern the country, wanted to perform and rule in their exclusive jurisdictions as well. They thought Ottawa was using shared-cost programs to enter provincial fields and alter their own spending priorities. The federal government's view, on the other hand, was that it had a duty to see that all Canadians, regardless of where they lived, had access to a uniform set of basic services. Ottawa even spearheaded three-way shared-cost programs, with the federal, provincial and municipal governments all co-operating in areas of obvious provincial jurisdiction, such as housing, public works, urban development and, as we shall see, infrastructure.

Although shared-cost programs in theory focused on defining and creating national standards for Canadians, their real effect was to end any generally accepted "standards" of financial accountability, in both theory and practice. Essentially the programs encouraged government to bypass parliamentary structures for monitoring and debating public-spending decisions. Today, in fact, we have many different types of shared-cost programs, including some in which the federal government and only a select few provinces participate. So much for the "national standards" argument! These programs include tourism development, manpower training, assistance to the blind and disabled, regional development and sewer and water-supply projects. (It is hard to imagine which Father of Confederation might ever have contemplated the Government of Canada being involved in building local sewers!) The provincial governments may have found it difficult to accept some of these programs, but they went along for quite a distance because even if Ottawa was in the driver's seat, the ride was half-fare.

The provincial governments signed on, changing their internal priorities and program administration accordingly. At the time few imagined that the deep pockets of the federal government would by the mid-1990s be so empty that Ottawa would unilaterally slash transfers by billions of dollars. If the provinces could have foreseen Finance Minister Paul Martin's 1995 federal budget back in the 1960s when they were first being enticed into these joint programs by Ottawa, few would have set themselves up for the devastating hit they took three decades later. You might argue that no one in government is capable of seeing that far into the future, but a number of provincial premiers did just that. The record robustly shows that Premier Roblin of Manitoba and Premier Robarts of Ontario were dragged and dragooned against their own best judgment into such programs. Roblin and Robarts understood the folly of the national government inserting itself as a full player in areas of provincial jurisdiction that were already being fully and competently administered. Yet in due course even they signed on to avoid losing their provinces' share of the funds flowing from Ottawa. Only Quebec — where opposition to Ottawa's breaking of the constitutional restraints of jurisdiction was more profound, deeply felt and closely reasoned — stood its ground. Quebec premiers, in particular Jean Lesage, found a way to receive the money Ottawa insisted on spending, while remaining "masters in their own house." Quebec "opted out" of the Government of Canada's programs, set up its own with comparable standards and got the money.

Opting out became a shared-cost alternative, a pragmatic way for those in government to contend with Canadian realities. To some Canadians with antipathy toward Quebec and anything French, opting out was seen as disloyal to the new mood in Canada, to the spirit of "Confederation on the March." Of course, in Quebec, where provincial governments of all stripes considered themselves in step with the

Constitution and believed it was Ottawa that was playing the wrong marching tune, opting out was seen not as disloyalty, but as fidelity to the compact of Confederation and the original constitutional agreement. Opting out has a different meaning depending on whether one is in the parade or watching it go by. From Quebec it looked like the rest of the country had entirely opted out of the Constitution itself. As Quebec remained firmly and securely planted upon its established constitutional ground, the rest of the country, under Ottawa's captaincy, sailed further and further from shore. In our paradoxical Canadian fashion, French-Canadian nationalists who ultimately were driven to seek a sovereign Quebec state and thereby break the Constitution were the least separatist of all, and the most loyal to the Constitution and its once accountable division of powers.

By 1965 Ottawa's new Established Programs (Interim Arrangements) Act gave all provinces the right to opt out of certain shared-cost programs. It was not hard to see why provinces would hesitate. The legislation covered several areas of provincial jurisdiction, including hospital insurance, vocational training and various social-welfare programs. The deal was that the Government of Canada would reduce federal income tax points in any province that opted out so that the province could raise its own tax rates to gain additional income to pay for its own version of these programs. Under the formula in the Established Programs Act, the additional income raised by the province is supposed to match the funds the province would have received from the national government under the shared-cost program. Only Quebec exercised the option. It was no coincidence that around this same time René Lévesque, pushed further and further toward separation, published his book entitled *Option Québec*.

Ottawa's final big jump was the Canada Assistance Plan. Introduced in 1966, it was one of the last major building blocks in the construction of Canada's welfare state under the government of Prime Minister Pearson. The plan, in essence, was a transfer payment writ large. It further changed the character of Canada's federal relations, giving the Government of Canada responsibility for paying half the costs of provincial-municipal social assistance. The plan was uniquely coherent because it replaced a multitude of national cost-sharing programs. Yet it also extended federal assistance into *additional* areas. It included providing assistance with necessities (food, shelter, clothing and fuel);

maintaining individuals in homes for the aged, nursing homes or child-care institutions; and rehabilitation, daycare, homemaker and adoption services. It would be a rare Canadian who would not support government helping those in need. However, the issue here is not *whether* government should be providing such services, but rather *which level* of government should be doing so. Since these are all matters of provincial and local concern, constitutionally falling under the clearly accountable jurisdiction of provincial government, why did Ottawa need to interfere? Whatever noble motives or political pressures may have triggered Ottawa's interference, however, the point here is not just that the Government of Canada waded into areas beyond its jurisdiction. Ours is an even larger point: it was this interference that blurred, irrevocably, the lines of accountability.

Ironically, many sincere people who have expressed anger about Ottawa's overspending and high taxes over the past several decades have been equally incensed by calls for the recognition of Quebec's distinctiveness within our country. They don't realize that there would be less debt on their backs in the first place if Ottawa had heeded Quebec's stubborn insistence that the federal government keep out of provincial jurisdiction. An emotional personal reaction has prevented many Canadians from recognizing the deeper erosion of a real and potentially effective check on expansive government spending. Quebec's consistent warnings should have alerted all Canadians that a constitutional safeguard was being systematically dismantled, undermined at the foundation though the superstructure still remained visible. The formal division of constitutional powers, in fact, is a legal reflection of the unique balance in our union between French-speaking and English-speaking Canadians. This arrangement was established 135 years ago at Confederation to ensure that the Government of Quebec would have jurisdiction over matters vital to the survival and success of Canada's French-speaking community, such as language, education, civil law and social services. This contract meant that every other provincial government, as well as the national government, would be responsible — and accountable — for respecting these clearly defined jurisdictions.

In practice our tendency for years has been to test the limits and the meanings of these jurisdictional boundaries. In the decades immediately following Confederation, for example, a series of constitutional court cases involving Ottawa and Ontario took place, over everything from which level of government controlled liquor manufacture and sale to which had jurisdiction over rivers. So Quebec wasn't the only province that pitted itself against the Government of Canada — but it was the Quebec government that, from the late 1940s into the early 1960s, opposed Ottawa's spending on higher education and universities. It was also during this period, between 1952 and 1953 to be exact, that the province decided to collect its own corporate taxes as a means of maintaining better control. Then, starting in 1960, instead of just standing up to the national government, Quebec started negotiating, and soon shared-cost programs began and opting out and parallel programs were developed. This series of events explains why the social safety net is much more decentralized in Quebec than elsewhere in Canada. The province has, for example, its own pension fund, tax system and family allowance.

As I've suggested, had Quebec's claim to these constitutional balances been respected, it would have prevented Ottawa from spending breathtaking amounts of money in provincial jurisdictions. Respect for the Constitution would have avoided duplication. It would have checked the runaway spending that contributed to building up the national debt. It would have saved French-Canadian nationalists from having to become Quebec separatists. Paule Gauthier, a Quebec City lawyer and past president of the Canadian Bar Association, explained it this way:

> The understanding of many Quebecers about why there is a deficit comes from the fact that there are too many levels of government. There are duplications of services and it's costly. They know that the federal government is involved, the province is involved, and they want that to disappear. For some the best way to settle this difficulty is to separate. Then you are sure you will only have one level of government.

Much of the effort that began in the 1960s to change our Constitution has proven largely counterproductive. Separatism, which most of these changes were intended to prevent, is incomparably stronger than it was at the start of the voyage. Attitudes of regional and cultural alienation within the country have been galvanized into powerful movements. These movements operate both inside and outside the structure of political parties in the country, and have influenced some which already existed and created additional new ones, such as the Parti

Québécois, Bloc Québécois, Confederation of Regions Party, the Western Canada Concept Party, the Reform Party and the Canadian Alliance. Such fragmenting of traditional political formations into many new ones is connected to the failure of older parties to uphold and respect the political responsibilities of our established constitutional arrangements. It also suggests why most Canadians are feeling increasingly alienated from the existing political system.

Is there any lesson to be learned by asking "What if?" I think so. For example, what if Ottawa had lived by the Constitution and respected Quebec's jurisdiction? Canadian history of the past 35 years could have been written differently. If a stricter interpretation of the division of constitutional powers had been adhered to, Ottawa's irresponsible spending would not — could not — have happened. If the message Quebec nationalists had been preaching had been sooner heeded, it would have actually aided the unity of Canada in the long term. Rather than witnessing Quebec's Quiet Revolution, the story would have been about *Canada's* Quiet Revolution. Instead, the history of our post-war era became a saga about the four horsemen of Canada's apocalypse — political stalemate, endless constitutional tinkering, financial crisis through overspending and lack of clear accountability.

Asking "What if...?" is important because the future is not a given; it is often decided by simple choices and small events that alter the course of history. Examining what might have been different in the past — if, say, constitutional accountability had been upheld — can also give insights about what is happening now. So let's fastforward to a contemporary example of this sort of constitutional tinkering. One only has to look at the Canada Infrastructure Works Program, a vast, three-level governmental spending program involving billions of dollars, countless private contractors and several years of construction and reconstruction projects in every nook and cranny of Canada. Between 1997 and 1999 researchers with the *underground royal commission* examined this infrastructure program in more detail than anyone else in the country. Their findings provide a current and tangible example of the kind of waste and mismanagement that can occur when jurisdictional responsibilities become blurred and institutional accountability is lost.

This story is all the more eloquent for its simplicity. The Chrétien Liberal government initiated the multilevel cost-sharing program early in 1994; it was designed to repair and upgrade the country's crumbling infrastructure, with each level of government (national, provincial, municipal) contributing one-third of the cost to each project. Ottawa justified its intrusion into provincial jurisdiction and municipal matters on the basis that water and sewage problems (which would form at least some part of the planned municipal public works upgrading projects) are really *pollution* issues, a national responsibility. However, this claim is somewhat dubious. Since the 1970s Ottawa has behaved as if pollution problems were part of its jurisdiction, but Section 109 of the Constitution gives provinces control of natural resources, and other sections clearly give the provinces control over environmental matters. It certainly can be argued on constitutional grounds that the national government was intended to stay out of this field in most respects. Yet doggedly consistent with its expansionist role in other areas of provincial responsibility, Ottawa's assertion that pollution had always been a matter of federal jurisdiction formed a mildly plausible basis for intervening in public works across the country.

Leading up to the 1988 general election, the Liberals, led by John Turner, claimed that if the problems of Canada's allegedly ailing infrastructure were not addressed, the cost to repair them later would greatly compound. This initiative was clearly intended to demonstrate a responsible attitude. Concerns about infrastructure not being something Ottawa could properly be involved in if it respected constitutional jurisdictions were simply overlooked. Again, just prior to the 1993 general election, the Liberals, now with new leader Jean Chrétien, adopted the same infrastructure platform, although by this time the estimated cost had soared, being hastily revised by the zealous municipal government lobbyists keen for the work!

It was in 1997 that researchers from the *underground royal commission* set out to review the infrastructure program in terms of government reporting, control and accountability. They assumed that because the infrastructure program had clearly stated and tangible goals — upgrading and repairing the country's crumbling infrastructure while creating jobs and enhancing the economy in the process — they could measure for accountability *in accordance with the program's own stated aims and purpose*. This task proved not to be so easy. The researchers did find examples of infrastructure overdue for maintenance or upgrading: sewers that could collapse at any moment, roads pock marked with dangerous potholes, bridges unable to sustain their current stress loads. Yet, strangely, when it came to handing out the infrastructure money, many of these projects were overlooked in favour of more high-profile, politically appealing endeavours, such as theatres and athletic facilities. Decision making for the projects had somehow become disconnected from the original project goals. The multibillion-dollar infrastructure project had been launched on the basis of a real need to repair sewers and build overpasses, but the political appeal of more culturally satisfying projects had proven irresistible.

A second problem emerged with the job claims. The federal government stated the program created over 120,000 jobs, based cumulatively on projections municipalities supplied of job numbers for a project. When the researchers tried to verify these numbers, however, they found that at the project (municipal) level, records were often poorly kept and numbers were occasionally padded. Job numbers were certainly open to question. That's only part of the picture. At the national level, the government had been continually releasing numbers on job creation to the media based upon the statistics coming from the municipalities — figures that were only *estimates* of the number of people the local governments thought would be required to do the work. Moreover, when the auditor general of Canada looked at the infrastructure program in the fall of 1996, he found major flaws in the way the federal government calculated the number of jobs created, reporting that the government statistics were probably off by as much as 35 percent. He found that much of the Canada Works spending was devoted to projects that were already slated to go ahead regardless of the infrastructure program, noting that about one-third of the jobs would have been created without the funding.

How could a program with such explicit and measurable goals get so far off track? The problem can be traced back to the way the program was implemented, and specifically, to the multilevel institutional structures improvised to administer the projects. Within eight weeks of the program being announced in early 1994, Ottawa had signed agreements with all 10 provinces, the territories and First Nations' peoples. These agreements established a process for receiving, reviewing and approving funding applications for public works projects. Although applications for local projects emerged from the municipal level, it was representatives of the provincial governments and Ottawa's regional development agencies across Canada who co-chaired the management committees.

These bodies, on which, astonishingly, there was little municipal representation, made all the spending decisions. Moreover, the procedures put in place to administer the program sidestepped traditional constitutional rules of jurisdiction and avoided the normal parliamentary structures of spending review, but tellingly, no counterpart tri-level structure or mechanism was established on the evaluation and financial-control side. At the national level, Parliament's Public Accounts Committee reviews federal expenditures. At the provincial level, a similar committee reviews provincial expenditures. Municipal governments operate a review process as well. Yet when the infrastructure program linked the three levels of government on the spending side, no matching institution for accountability was correspondingly established. In this way, the Canada Infrastructure Works Program actually institutionalized a structural and functional absence of accountability.

The infrastructure program had been fast-tracked, implemented through structures that were both new to and separate from the normal channels of government. (In the case of the Canada-Quebec infrastructure agreement, reference to the Financial Administration Act, found in agreements with other provinces, was notably absent — a portent, perhaps, of the problem Auditor General Sheila Fraser would identify in May 2002, when she found that senior civil servants in Ottawa had violated this statute in relation to service contracts in Quebec. She turned the matter over to the RCMP and launched a further government-wide value-for-money audit of all similar contracts.) The result was sobering: although huge amounts of money were poured into these projects, it was entirely unclear who — or even which level of government — was actually responsible for making spending decisions. Officials had only to satisfy *themselves* that the projects met the guidelines of the infrastructure program and that there were dollars available. While in theory the files were open for inspection, there was no requirement to report. "There's nobody in reality who's clearly identified as the person responsible for the program from a political or even administrative point of view," admitted Tully Clifford, manager of Calgary Transportation Services, "You could point a finger, but it would be at nobody."

It may seem ironic that municipalities, the level of government presumably most qualified to identify local infrastructure needs, usually had little input in terms of which projects would get funding. Vancouver councillor George Puil, for example, revealed that municipalities in

British Columbia were not involved in deciding which projects were necessary: "The projects that were done were the projects that the various MLAs, MPs or the provincial government wanted done — not what the city felt was necessary." Because federal and provincial politicians could more easily attract publicity and increase their visibility by securing funding for projects like bike paths and theatres (as opposed to sewer or road repairs), many of the approved projects had nothing at all to do with core infrastructure. The result was that many cities received funding for projects they neither needed nor had asked for, but got little or no money to upgrade infrastructure that was literally falling apart and which had formed the basis of their applications in the first place. In Toronto Councillor Jack Layton explained that the sudden appearance of this large pot of money from Ottawa, which had to be quickly spent, threw municipal priorities off balance. Former Ontario NDP cabinet minister Ruth Grier described how the structure and operation of this program skewed the priorities of the province and "overall probably ranked only four or five out of 10 as a success."

Whatever Canadians had been publicly told by governments about the value of the multibillion-dollar Canada Works project, insiders knew the truth. The Soberman Report, commissioned by the Government of Canada to evaluate the efficacy of the program, concluded that the jobs it created resulted in only "modest improvements in the economy." Far more damning, the report also determined that the government could have created more jobs by putting the money toward daycare centres, an investment that also would have benefited the country's youth in the long term. The report additionally concluded that if the infrastructure funding had been used to, say, pay down part of the national debt, it would have had the same impact on the economy. It strongly recommended that the government *not* embark on any renewal or extension of the infrastructure program. Nevertheless, just six months before the 1997 general election, Prime Minister Chrétien topped up the program with another $1.4 billion; the Canada Infrastructure Works Program had already been stretched over five years (from its initial two) and now totalled $6 billion at the national level alone. By this point, of course, nobody was even asking about the constitutional division of powers that found Ottawa building bicycle paths and bocce courts. (For more detail on the infrastructure program, including the findings of the Soberman Report, see three other books in the *underground royal commission* series: *Down the Road Never Travelled* by Brigitte Pellerin; *Secrets in High Places* by Jay Innes; and *On the Money Trail* by Tim Chorney with Jay Innes.)

Looking at the infrastructure program in terms of accountability, many issues leap out. Jurisdictionally, which level of government is responsible for what types of infrastructure? Procedurally, who decides which projects are more important than others? Administratively, how are the contracts for these projects supervised and costs controlled? The answers should depend upon a combination of what the Constitution and administrative law stipulate and what Canadians need and are prepared to pay for. What was discovered, however, was that when it came to making almost any of these decisions, the Canada Infrastructure Works Program simply paved over accountability. If this is how government operates under a relatively simple program such as this, can accountability be any better in more complex areas of long-standing multilevel governmental activity, such as health care, environment, education or security?

In theory, finding accountability should be easy in a self-governing democracy. Yet considering the evidence from our recent history, we must ask ourselves this question. If we *gain* accountability through constitutional institutions such as federalism, isn't this precisely the same place where we can *lose* it? The long-smouldering issues behind Quebec nationalism and contemporary projects such as the Canada Infrastructure Works Program demonstrate, from different angles, how the most fundamental bulwarks of accountability have been eroded. Indeed, the Constitution itself has been virtually abandoned as a functioning framework for accountability. Yet because its form and structures endure, even if its substance does not, Canadians have been left, perversely, with a system of government that now manages to institutionalize this very lack of accountability.

4. Spending Controls

When Financial Accountability Became a Fiction Too

Spending money is how government expresses and implements policy. If money talks, this is how government speaks. The concept of spending controls is premised on the notion that, given finite government resources, choices must be made. Indeed, spending controls are designed to force choice through specifically limiting the money available to government agencies, departments and programs. However, such controls are also intended to ensure that these choices are made in an environment of transparency — under the watchful eye of citizens, journalists and Parliament. When spending controls disintegrate, so too does financial accountability.

To speak of choice is another way of describing the concept of opportunity cost. Economists use the term "opportunity cost" to express the value of the choice we have made as the maximum benefit derived from selecting the next best alternative. For example, if you spend $2 million on military equipment, it's money not available for health care or education, and vice versa. The opportunity cost of spending $2 million on military equipment is, therefore, the health-care or education improvements that we forego in choosing to spend limited resources in this manner.

Spending choices, coupled with accountability, measure how responsible we are about getting closer to the goals we've set for ourselves, as individuals or as a country. So examining governmental accountability and the relevance of Parliament to this decision-making process is really a way to measure how realistic our contemporary Canadian system is about handling the ethics of choice when faced with such tradeoffs. It is even a good way to see how adept Canadian political culture is at handling hard choices. That is why we owe it to ourselves to explore the role of public trust and evaluate the nature of political efficiency in our Canadian methods of governance. The way hard choices get handled — whether they are dealt with in a methodical, cost-effective and transparent manner — is another way to approach the issue of accountability.

Even as far back as the 1920s some politicians recognized that our parliamentary ways and the pressures of immediate political interests prevented the House of Commons from effectively evaluating spending decisions as economic choices with long-term implications. In England Winston Churchill proposed, in a speech to students at Oxford University, the creation of an ongoing "economic sub-Parliament." It would be an additional body, a new part of an existing institution that could consider, debate and evaluate economic policies free from the political constraints and partisan pressures housed within the Commons and the corridors of power inhabited by Cabinet ministers and senior civil servants. However, the British never adopted Churchill's sub-Parliament idea, and neither did we — in Canada economic policy still dwells at the very heart of government operations and the political process, and spending decisions are often made without sufficient analysis, evenhanded evaluation or public understanding of the opportunity costs involved. The result is that we have many examples of the ways in which we pay for missed opportunities. For example, when the Canada Infrastructure Works Program spends money on theatres and bike paths, it does so at *the expense of* the next best alternative (sewers, roads and rebuilt bridges).

What we've been exploring in this book is the fact that the available resources involved in an opportunity-cost situation are being treated as if they're infinite (for example, going into debt, running a deficit) rather than finite. So what we've seen, in turn, is the failure to make choices and initiate an *open* discussion of necessary opportunity costs. Instead there has simply been a decades-long deluge of stories about wasteful government spending. We learned about programs that were intended to achieve results (such as eliminating regional economic disparities or child poverty) but did just the opposite. We witnessed government using taxes and heavy borrowing which, according to former auditor general Maxwell Henderson, "sap[ped] the incentive of our people." We discovered we had amassed a staggering national debt, with billions of dollars needed each year just to pay the interest charges.

For many decades most Canadians assumed that the debt didn't matter, that we both should and could keep having all our existing programs and services from government. If citizens felt this way, it was hardly surprising. This was also the outlook of many — indeed most — in government itself. If there wasn't enough money to pay the bills as they fell due, we could simply borrow to cover the shortfall. So borrow we did, as much as $60 billion a year. It seemed for a while in the 1960s and 1970s that we could have the world's best welfare state, for individuals and corporations alike, without worrying about the economy. Yet 40 percent of our national debt had come to be held by foreigners, then 50 percent. Foreign investors were rapidly losing interest in continuing to buy our government bonds, so we had to keep jacking up the interest rates we'd pay on the borrowed money to make the bonds more enticing. Canadian financial houses that sought to place government bonds with investors kept quiet about the overall financial picture of the country, which was deteriorating, and instead pocketed their commission fees on the sales. By the early 1990s the bond rating companies dropped the credit ratings of many of our governments. The country could no longer afford to keep borrowing, to continue living on the credit of tomorrow, and we passed through a painful period of government cutbacks and service reductions. By the late 1990s many Canadians began to think that the slightly improving health of public finances and the gradual improvement in several provinces' credit ratings meant that the earlier problem had been licked. Anyone who believed that did not know what the original problem truly was. The national debt is just the symptom of a deeper crisis in governance. A more penetrating look will give a better understanding of what was really going on.

To start, let's go back to when public finances were sound and administrative procedures accountable, in that period immediately after the Second World War. At this time government had a carefully devised agenda. When it became clear in 1944 that the war was going to end, planning began in earnest for the post-war years. "The really great determination — and this was with *unanimity*, like the wartime unanimity — was that there must never again be the kind of economic and human situation we had had during the 10 years of the 1930s," explained Gordon Robertson, who served as clerk of the Privy Council in both the Pearson and Trudeau governments and experienced first hand the philosophical shifts in government thinking that occurred while these two prime ministers were in office (a span of nearly 20 years). "It's absolutely vital to understand that thinking or you can't understand what was done after the war." The fundamental attitude toward post-war spending was to avoid an economic letdown, an economic recession of the kind there had been after World War I. "We did avoid any significant economic recession. We did avoid unemployment," said Robertson, indicating the policy was indeed a success. Yet there was something more: "Spending, the attitude toward spending, was that to the extent it was necessary to achieve those purposes, it was going to be done."

During the war the Government of Canada had already moved into a position of directing and leading domestic affairs in ways it never had before, creating industries where none existed, allocating natural and human resources toward clearly defined national goals. Equally important, this marked the period when senior government planners began laying the foundations for a significant new approach in economic policy. Canada was among the very first countries to implement Keynesian economics, and Robert Bryce, who studied at Cambridge (home university of John Maynard Keynes) had subsequently spread the Keynesian gospel at Harvard before returning home to Canada and senior policy positions in government in Ottawa. Keynes himself was in Ottawa in 1942 to help develop the application of his ideas in our country.

Under the Keynesian approach, instead of passively watching the cycles of boom and bust — those hallmarks of capitalist economics caused by the supply-and-demand flows and forces of the open market — government would now intervene to smooth out the ups and downs.

It would spend in times of economic downturn to stimulate the economy and create jobs, even if it had to borrow money to do so. The corollary was that in prosperous times government would recoup revenue from the booming economy to pay off the debt it had incurred in the previous cycle. By the late 1960s, however, the government had forgotten this second part of the formula. Those running the governments in Canada (for provinces, too, had moved to Keynesian economics) as well as citizens making larger spending claims upon the public purse were seduced by the easy pleasures of spending and put off the harsher task of paying down the (supposedly) short-term debt. Once economic conditions in the country began booming, everyone felt confidently prosperous again and the idea of repaying the debt seemed almost irrelevant and certainly not, for a number of years in the 1970s, very important. In the case of an individual, this might be understandable. Yet the government? Hadn't it put into place any tripwire mechanisms, structures or laws to ensure that such an obvious problem would not occur, to ensure accountability to the dual requirements of the Keynesian approach? It had not.

Nevertheless, for a long period the government's interventionist approach and higher levels of spending seemed to be working, tempering the harshness of raw market forces and sweetening the bitterness of capitalism. Ottawa felt vindicated; those in power had found a way to carry out their steely resolve that Canadians would not again suffer the economic depredation of the Dirty Thirties. Government's role in this new order as a means of achieving a strong economy and a fair society was assured. Champions of new political, social and economic policies for post-war Canada felt no discomfort at all with the idea that government would take a leading role in creating a better society. They advocated with compelling arguments that it should. Most Canadians, having seen how the government could handily marshal resources for the war effort, were fully prepared to accept this new state of affairs. Even so, our thinking still seemed to be split on the topic of money. It was as if one side of the public brain believed money was of no particular concern, that just as government had found vast funds to build a war machine, it could now likewise find money for peace-time purposes. The Keynesian idea to "keep money in circulation" and keep the engines of the economy humming made sense to us intuitively. The other side of the public brain, however, thought that frugality was still a virtue, indebtedness the source of ruin. Even with this dichotomy of views, our attitude about spending money on a big scale was markedly different than it had been in earlier times. In this post-war era money was not so much a measurement of wealth as it was a tool of public policy. We were in the process of developing a new way of thinking, and it called for a re-evaluation of our previously restrictive and frugal values.

The consequences of these trends, new economic theories and changed policies began to show up in a number of ways. From the mid-1960s to the mid-1980s Canada's emerging welfare state, providing welfare for both individuals and corporations, expanded at a very generous pace. This expansion was a direct result of larger governments at all levels flexing newfound muscles; but it was also a clear expression of the popular belief that government could solve the major problems of society and ought to do so. Over time a generous and limitless view of the capacity of government came to be held by both our elected representatives and the general public. As we have already seen, the ensuing spending juggernaut extended into areas where governments had not realized previously that they could busy themselves. The result was relentless growth of three related areas: the number of government programs and services available to the country's citizens and businesses; the size and role of the public service; and, in the 1970s, large-scale peacetime deficit financing.

This overview of Canada at mid-20th century is not enough, however, to understand the root causes of our massive debt load. For that we need to examine the mechanisms and structures that are supposed to make government accountable for its spending decisions, which brings us back to Parliament. Parliament gets to see the government's spending plans in advance in order to scrutinize, debate and, if appropriate, authorize them. Spending is projected department by department in the Estimates. These voluminous documents list all the programs and services of government, then show for each one, line by line, the anticipated expenses for the coming fiscal year. From housing on Indian reserves to new helicopters for the Canadian Armed Forces to computers for government offices, the list of spending categories goes on and on, into billions and billions of dollars — the envy of procurement officers and power shoppers everywhere. Only once Parliament has approved the Estimates can spending occur. This is Parliament's most central and historic function, summed up as "control of the public purse strings."

That's the theory. In practice, over the past 40 years the government's financial functionaries began to proceed on the assumption that parliamentary scrutiny and debate were simply a formality, that Parliament would always approve the spending. Indeed, as the amounts got bigger, the minds of MPs grew increasingly numb and approvals did seem to come more easily.

So government kept operating, day in, day out, a perpetual-motion spending machine. Parliament usually did approve the Estimates, although sometimes it took quite a while. In the 1960s and early 1970s parliamentary sessions would drag on into the sweltering heat of Ottawa's summer, with MPs still studying and debating the Estimates when many wanted to be back home in their ridings or at the lake or cottage. So to make Parliament more "efficient," the Trudeau Liberal government changed the House rules in 1972: departmental estimates had to be approved by June 23 each year; if they had not been, they would be "deemed" approved anyway. This rule effectively made the role of parliamentary approval a sham. It hollowed out Parliament's raison d'être by removing the most effective control the people's representatives had in holding government accountable. Parliamentarians who endorsed this radical surgery thought it was a good idea at the time, even calling it a "reform." Yet they had given it thought from an efficiency point of view, not from the perspective of institutional effectiveness in terms of accountability over time. (Nobody seems to have thought about simply changing the government's fiscal year so that Parliament could thoroughly debate spending during the long, dark winter rather than during one of the few hot-weather months of the year.) Thirty years later even the strongest proponents of the 1972 restructuring are dismayed by the distorting consequences it wrought upon spending control and accountability in government. Senator John Stewart from Nova Scotia was an MP from 1962–1968, and he chaired the parliamentary committee that recommended the change. He told researchers for the *underground royal commission* that he felt, at the time, that a more selective focus on a few departments each year would enable members of Parliament to examine policies and spending priorities more thoroughly and become more effective. He also expressed regret that the implemented reforms did not work out the way he envisioned.

Nor was it easy for MPs who wanted to be thorough in reviewing departmental spending plans to really understand the public accounts. Paul Dick, an MP who subsequently served in the Mulroney Cabinet, had made a cause out of trying to comprehend the unintelligible financial records of the federal government. He even convened a committee of six heads of the top chartered accounting firms in Ottawa to review the public accounts. "Five of the six said they could not understand them," revealed Dick. "One did, but he added that he'd worked in government." The financial records by which an MP would seek to understand what was going on were being kept in a "third official language" which nobody really understood. Yet the practice has not changed, and for 30 years departmental spending plans for the Government of Canada have effectively been given automatic approval.

Over this period, as government spending inevitably and inexorably rose, the Estimates were each year accompanied by ever-larger borrowing bills. These allowed the government to seek parliamentary approval to put the country further into debt. At that point the choice became quite clear: government could either cut spending or borrow more money to make up the shortfall. Some very interesting reasons emerged to explain why the choice should be "spend and borrow" rather than "cut and save." Only a few voices could be heard protesting that we were losing financial accountability. The government insisted, through party discipline, that government MPs line up in favour of these bills because they were "budgetary measures" and therefore confidence votes that if lost would mean defeat of the government itself under our doctrine of responsible government.

Changes in the internal administrative methods, meanwhile, continued apace. As government expanded its activities through more programs and operations, it introduced further "efficiency" reforms. For one, it decided to lump together many more individual spending programs in the Estimates. Items that had once been scrutinized, discussed and voted on one by one were now jumbled together and approved as a group. As such, a single item being voted on could now easily be authorizing many millions of dollars in spending. They say "the devil is in the details," but that's also where accountability resides. This amalgamation of so much substantive information meant that important details were submerged and lost. Out of sight, out of mind.

Of course, Parliament isn't the only safeguard of accountability. Other institutional tripwires had been created over time to help Parliament control the public purse strings, namely the comptroller general (whose job was to rein in spending before it took place) and the auditor general (who reviewed and reported on spending after it had occurred). Their reports to Parliament enhanced MPs' ability to evaluate government spending. With their staffs and expertise, comptrollers and auditors could delve deeper into the public accounts and perform a more detailed analysis than any individual MP or even a parliamentary caucus researcher would be able to do. Yet in the 1960s and 1970s the government reduced the powers of the comptroller general through administrative and procedural changes recommended by the Glassco Report, released in 1962. The report urged government to "let the managers manage" by getting rid of financial-approval bottlenecks in the administrative process. The function of the comptroller general was transferred to Treasury Board and essentially gutted; a Cabinet minister would now preside over the office. Today the comptroller general is still on the scene in name, which is great for appearances, but this official is no longer the powerful spending guardian of former years. Indeed, after the role of the comptroller general was diminished, the problem of rising government expenditures worsened demonstrably.

Meanwhile, the size and function of the Office of the Auditor General became more notable as the size of government operations, which it exists to audit, expanded. As an officer of Parliament who reports to Parliament through the minister of finance, the auditor general conducts an annual audit of government spending to see whether

- proper accounts are being kept;
- money is being spent for the purposes stipulated by Parliament;
- effective spending controls are being maintained;
- money designated for one purpose is not being diverted to another;
- all money collected from the public is properly accounted for;
- proper inventories are being kept of public property; and

- generally accepted accounting procedures are being followed by government departments and agencies.

The auditor general's annual report to Parliament on all these points is reviewed by the Public Accounts Committee, which is chaired by an Opposition MP to help ensure a more critical eye is brought to government spending. This report, keenly awaited by the opposition parties and news media and apprehensively anticipated by the government, itemizes instances of misspending or lack of adequate financial controls. The multimillion-dollar spending and grants scandal at Human Resources Development Canada in 1999 and 2000, for example, first came to public attention through reports of the auditor general. Another example occurred in May 2002, when Auditor General Sheila Fraser reported on three sponsorship contracts the federal government had signed with Montreal advertising firm Groupaction; in each case the government did not receive what it had contracted for (sponsorship opportunities in Quebec) even though it paid $1.6 million to the company. Fraser concluded that laws, including the Financial Administration Act, had been broken by civil servants and contracting rules had been violated. She also called in the RCMP for further police investigation of the matter (the RCMP exceed her powers of office and can subpoena documents and interview people outside government) and launched a government-wide value-for-money audit of all such sponsorship contracts to see if this corruption was endemic throughout the system.

Reports of the auditor general often contain recommendations on ways to improve financial procedures within the government or point to improvements which have been carried out from previous years in response to earlier recommendations. The role of the auditor general is greatly affected by responsive behaviour — indeed, that is what this official's work is intended to engender. As an after-the-fact evaluator, however, the auditor general does not exercise control over spending; he or she merely reports on funds once they have been disbursed. That is why the comptroller general, who could hold up spending in advance if there was not enough money available, was in significant and practical ways much more important, and perhaps why this office was more thoroughly and sooner eviscerated. If there is any control in the auditor general's work at all, it lies in the hope that shocking revelations of past practices and the news media's hunger for more might make government keen to mend its ways and get greater value for money in the future. Yet even this has proved to be a faint hope.

Instead, the government has mostly responded in quite a different fashion — by trying to control the political damage caused by media attention and silence its critics. For example, Maxwell Henderson, appointed auditor general in 1960, explained how he "exposed so much government waste and extravagance over the years and got such tremendous press doing it" that in no time at all he became a folk hero. That put him "on a collision course" with the Trudeau government: "They decided to make my life difficult, and they proceeded with a series of events that did just that, downsizing the salaries of my men, freezing my staff and trying to prevent me from disclosing so much in my reports." It was nothing less than a full-scale power struggle about financial accountability.

Having the staff and expertise to help Parliament scrutinize government spending practices is key to the auditor general's role, but the true challenge of that role itself, quite apart from organized resistance and intimidation from the government, really emerges when the hidden nature of those spending records is appreciated. This is not like looking at the books of a retail store, or for that matter auditing the financial records of any of Canada's biggest publicly traded business operations. Government accounting practices involve such an uncontrollable and unaccountable maze of entries and payments that money can go missing and nobody knows where it went. When the CBC "lost" some $50 million one year, all we got was a shrug and a mind-numbing explanation that it was a "paper trail loss." In 2002 Canadians learned that Ottawa had accidentally paid an extra $3.3 billion to a number of provinces. Had anybody noticed? The overpayments — on taxes collected by the Government of Canada for the provinces between 1993 and 1999 — had gone undetected until December 2001, when the error was revealed "during a computer system upgrade."

A revealing example of the accountability quagmire came when the *underground royal commission* researchers decided to look at the spending patterns in another way — by examining the lists of individuals, organizations or companies getting money from the Government of Canada in some form of subsidy. Several weeks later, after calls to Treasury Board, days in the reference library, more days on the computer, and still even more days tracing through the Estimates and public accounts, the researchers concluded that it was an impossible task. They began to suspect no one had ever tried to find this out before. They reported that the public accounts were "very difficult to understand, not very transparent, not very specific in talking about which moneys were going where." They weren't even trying to follow the path of a dollar all the way through government, just piece together basic information on specific payments to particular organizations! Part of the problem is that classification descriptions and recording protocols vary from one part of government to another; the same organization may receive funding from several different departments under separate programs, and the public accounts do not reveal in any reasonable or realistic fashion how many such payments or how much money in total that organization obtained.

All this is just a quick way of saying that the task of getting the public finances in order is probably the single overriding challenge for Canada as a self-governing country. Why? I repeat: money is policy. What it gets spent on or cut from is a direct expression of government policy and planning. A great deal of Canadian public policy, therefore, is in a state of confusion, and has been for quite some time now. The public accounts hold a mirror to that reality. Canada is not an efficient society in matters of governance because it is not an accountable society in terms of government.

Over the past decades it has been hard to get even those officials most directly responsible to take dire financial warnings seriously. Senior civil servants in Ottawa knew only too well how Robert Bryce, when deputy minister of finance in the early 1970s, had made the effort. At a Cabinet committee meeting Bryce discussed with the ministers the extent of the total financial load being taken on in various programs and spending commitments. He told the committee, "Ministers, you can do all of these things, but you cannot do them all at the same time." Bryce saw the financial load was getting heavier than the economy could stand. The problem with that sort of assertion, however, is that one cannot point to anything specific and say, "See, that proves it!" There is no clear proof. There was no way to demonstrate at that time that the burden of debt was in fact getting too heavy. It was like an informed or instinctive feeling. Senior officials appeared deaf to such warnings partly because they remembered that the country had incurred a staggering debt during World War II but paid it off almost entirely in about 15 years using budgetary surpluses specifically earmarked for this purpose. How could Robert Bryce prove this was serious, that the debt was now reaching the point where it could no longer be handled?

This lack of coherence in the management of public money and in the implementation of policy, and the concomitant lack of responsibility in the operation of government itself, has today taken on more virulent and institutionalized forms. In April 2002 Sheila Fraser reported to the House of Commons her concerns about the limited exposure to parliamentary scrutiny of a vast area of new government spending arrangements. Beginning in 1999 the auditor general had been monitoring and reporting on two ways the government is now putting public money out of Parliament's sight operationally. First are the "collaborative arrangements" in which the federal government is a partner with provincial and municipal governments, non-governmental organizations and the private sector in delivering programs such as Canada Infrastructure Works. The second are "delegated arrangements," set up as separate legal organizations to exercise discretionary authority in redistributing public money using public assets or delivering public services on the government's behalf. The Canadian Adaptation and Rural Development Fund is one example. The 1999 audit found serious weaknesses in the governing framework of these new arrangements, detailing the ways "accountability to Parliament was placed at risk unnecessarily."

The auditor general found some 77 such arrangements operating outside normal departmental jurisdictions in 1999, with the Government of Canada contributing a total of $26.2 billion to them between 1990 and 1999. She noted that because these delegated arrangements are established as non-profit corporations operating at arm's length from the government, "their accountability to Parliament is in question." Between 1996 and 2001, for example, the government paid $7.1 billion through transfers to nine foundations for policy objectives such as encouraging innovation, assisting students with post-secondary education costs and developing information technology systems for health care. Although the government treated the $7.1 billion as an expenditure, by the end of the fiscal year 2001 "almost the entire amount was still in the bank accounts and other investments of the foundations. Very little of it had actually been received by the ultimate intended recipients, namely the innovators, students and health-care providers."

When the government plays with taxpayer money this way, it's little wonder that it seeks mechanisms to place public funds beyond the scrutiny of Parliament. Limited exposure to Parliament is a problem from the outset. A majority of the delegated arrangements were not created by legislation. Only the Canada Millennium Scholarship Foundation, the Canada Foundation for Innovation and the Canada Foundation for Sustainable Development Technology had been created by special acts, debated and passed by Parliament. "Direct legislation," noted Fraser, "is a way to tailor the design of an organization and facilitate good governance and accountability," enabling Parliament to determine the mandate, governance and accountability provisions of the arrangement and retain control. Generally, the whole story of these separate government operations is disconnected from Parliament. None of the organizations files a corporate plan with Parliament and few submit annual reports to Parliament. The auditor general concluded that "in the delegated arrangements we examined, reporting to Parliament is not adequate for parliamentary scrutiny. Weak oversight of such arrangements is limiting ministers' answerability to Parliament. Parliament is not receiving reports on independent, broad-scope audits that examine more than the financial statements of delegated arrangements, including compliance with authorities, propriety and value for money."

We say that government has power. What this means in practice is that government has money to spend. The decision to spend money on one thing but not on another is the power of making choices with far-reaching implications for our lives. The irony is that overspending at first makes government appear more powerful than it really is and then later, because of its indebtedness, become weaker than it ought to be. The further unfortunate fact is that the tripwires of responsible government, for example, the Office of the Comptroller General and parliamentary approval of the Estimates — safeguards that reduced the likelihood of irresponsible spending or overspending and thus once helped to maintain the integrity of government — were diminished to the point where they were no longer effective or relevant. As a result, financial accountability disappeared and spending levels soared. Since the system could no longer connect cause with effect, it was no longer capable of being accountable. This ability of the government to spend without regard for any meaningful and integrated kind of accountability has, as we shall see, allowed for the increased power of lobbyists and the perversion of the concept of "public interest."

Where We Are Today

5. Why Applying a "Public Interest" Test Is Now Meaningless

The reality of how our system of self-government works, as we've seen under the microscope of accountability, is significantly different than the governing formalism and political rhetoric of our country may lead people to believe. Many may take exception to some of the analysis or want to debate some of the conclusions I've reported, but few Canadians any longer would, I think, doubt that "responsible government" is a misnomer to describe the functioning of public affairs in our country. Coming to such a conclusion is, frankly, deeply saddening.

Unfortunately even this is not the end of surprises, as far as accountability goes. For now we move ahead to gauge the impact of lost government accountability on people. Up to this point in the book we have conducted a systemic critique of such relatively austere topics as the Constitution, federal-provincial relations, auditors and comptrollers and infrastructure projects. Now we turn to consequences. The first of these consequences is the demolition of the concept of the "public interest"; the second the system's immunity to change; and the third the hollowing out of Parliament, where rituals rather than realities of accountability are observed.

We speak, sometimes rather grandly, of "representative government" in Canada to refer to our MPs elected to Parliament to represent us in the councils of the nation, but we've also seen, both in examples discussed up to now and no doubt in our own impressions of the role being performed by most representatives, that this idea is to be taken with a grain of salt. Yet just because elected representatives have for a variety of causes been rendered ineffectual, does not mean that representation does not occur. It does, but it takes the form of representations being made to government officials directly by the affected individuals and organizations, often through the intermediaries known as "lobbyists" and other advocates purporting to act in the public interest, rather than through the open parliamentary process. Many MPs see themselves as lobbyists for interests in their constituency and, somewhat pathetically, have come indeed to use this very term in describing their role. Even prime ministers have used this concept to explain their high-level interventions to get dubious "development grants" for golf courses, canoe museums, country inns and the like. Governing is thus reduced to managing access to the public trough, an exercise in which the premium is placed on rewarding those who support the government rather than on financial accountability.

The concept of the public interest may be an abstraction, but it is one that in the past has helped us to elevate the plans and actions of government above the level of personalities, self-interested politics and personal greed. The idea that management and development of the public domain should be for the public benefit calls upon government to establish conditions which ensure that a reasonable share of any increased value goes to the people as a whole. This requirement recognizes the higher importance of the entire community over individuals or particular organizations, especially when it comes to tradeoffs of benefits or advantages. The concept is to seek "the greatest good of the greatest number." However, this ill-defined idea of a public interest, though noble, still leaves lots of room for interpretation and application. That is where lobbying once again comes in — to provide timely meaning by spinning the notion of public interest to cover whatever wants or needs to be done.

As citizens we organize ourselves into many different groups, some of which inevitably are rivals in interest and outlook. Sometimes we may not even realize that our own membership in one organization is counted elsewhere for purposes of lobbying. For example, because of an affiliation agreed to by the leaders of the United Church Women and the National Action Committee on the Status of Women (NAC), a woman in a local congregation of the United Church of Canada would be counted among the hundreds of thousands of NAC "members," regardless of whether or not she agreed with NAC's aims or objectives. Or, as Sean Moore, Ottawa guru of lobbying and long-time monitor of the process told researchers for the *underground royal commission,* "You sign up with the Canadian Automobile Association to get their roadside service, and all of a sudden you're unwittingly part of their lobby for lower gas prices." In short, the presence and structure of institutionalized lobbying in Canada is greater than most people perhaps appreciate. The distracting front-man role of MPs helps disguise this from citizens.

Parliamentary politics is — or should be — all about balancing contending interests, trying in an acceptable and open process to evaluate them and decide on the best course of action. Politics is essentially a balancing act, and in a democratic society like ours the further issue, beyond artfully finding the right tradeoff point, is the degree to which this balancing is done in public view or behind closed doors. Most of the give and take is done "in camera," or out of public view, and this is where lobbying comes in yet again. Lobbying can refer to any organized attempt by a special-interest group to persuade government to do something or, for that matter, to refrain from doing something. Lobbying to influence government decisions and to produce the outcome you want sometimes requires a new law, program or policy. Sometimes it requires the maintenance of existing programs, perhaps with a slight adjustment. The issues involved often include spending of government funds. Lobbying touches upon taxation, regulatory rules, licensing, appointments to public offices, subsidies and enforcement of rules and regulations. Timely information and good contacts are vital elements to anyone engaged in this business. Lobbying is all about advancing interests in ways that generally are not open to public scrutiny, pushing in a way that does not seek in any evenhanded fashion the greatest good of the greatest number. Although lobbying seeks maximum benefits for the special-interest group in question, lobbyists invariably claim that by granting the concession they seek, government would be acting "in the public interest." Accordingly, the term "public interest" is by no means the altar of virtue that it pretends to be. Rather this phrase is increasingly used to mask the more questionable motives behind "special interests."

This process of influencing government involves numerous players and a variety of procedures or methods. Since 1945 an ever-increasing number of interest groups have become involved in Canadian political life, attempting to influence government policy and insinuate themselves into decision-making practices. More and more, these groups have formed direct relationships with government, bypassing the political parties through which particular interests formerly expressed themselves. In Canada lobbying is no longer focused on legislators; instead lobbyists appeal to senior civil servants and Cabinet ministers, who have the real say in the content of legislation before it gets into the fairly predictable routines of parliamentary ratification. This trend is one of several factors that has contributed to a "hollowing out" of the political parties — making them less the policy vehicles they once were and more mechanisms for raising money to win elections so as to be in office where they can better serve this brokerage machine. It has, in the process, created debate over the extent to which lobbyists are shadowy characters or legitimate actors in the Canadian democratic system.

Lobbying is not illegal in Canada, although bribery and corruption of public officials are, and influence peddling is likewise a crime. All are hard to prove because of the difficulty of getting evidence of collusion. The players are generally skilled and their transactions privately conducted, even though the business itself ultimately concerns the interests of the Canadian public. There are many types of lobbying, and lobbyists are considered by law to be bonafide. Most industry groups maintain staffs to influence government decision making and politicians; so do unions, cultural organizations and groups concerned with social-welfare policies. Lobbying practices range from the formal presentation of briefs to government, through personal meetings with politicians and civil servants, on to mail-in campaigns, entertainment and other seductive social activities.

The propriety of lobbying, even when legal, is an ethical issue in a democratic state. Some observers recognize that lobbying can be a constructive exercise because it provides information, contacts and alternative perspectives. This view would hold that lobbying entails just another stream of information for decision makers to consider. Other observers have a concern that lobbying invariably reflects ulterior motives and that the process is neither benign nor the "information" neutral. Lobbyists advocate their clients' interests before officials, committees and regulatory agencies, supplying detailed information on complex issues spun or shaped to the advantage of their paying clients. One only lobbies because one has a personal stake in the matter or is being paid to do it, or both. Today lobbying is where the real play and interaction with government occur, and the lobbyist has taken over the mediating role once played by political parties and the intermediary function of MPs.

For their part, professional lobbyists — the "hired guns" who sell their influence to high-paying clients with special interests — walk a fine line, especially when viewed in terms of our fundamental concept of responsible government. Openness in the conduct of public affairs is a way of ensuring accountability, and lobbying is therefore, by both definition and practice, seldom accountable. Lobbyists persuade their clients to believe they have special access to the powers-that-be, can provide them with information not readily available to others and can obtain favourable decisions and good results — outcomes that clients would not get if they pursued their interests through the open channels of government available to regular citizens. At the same time a clever lobbyist must lead government officials to believe that the proposal being made, the change in the rules being sought or the contract to be awarded really has to be done the way the lobbyist is pitching rather than the way the government was intending to proceed in the normal course of serving the public interest. Understandably, given the duplicitous nature of this dialogue, such conversations are not routinely held in a public arena or under the scrutiny of the news media.

The idea central to this murky enterprise is interference. Lobbyists try to get a person to make or refrain from making a particular decision. To pull this off they must alter the information — or the interpretation of information — upon which the decision maker will act. Effective lobbyists know how to work through and around the system. This is made much easier because of the many unco-ordinated and competing levels and branches of government, most of which are no longer subject to close scrutiny or any form of accountability that integrates the larger picture, for reasons we've already discussed. Professional lobbyist Jack Slibar, for example, described for the *underground royal commission* his experience in going from one branch that refused a request to another that would grant it — revealing how easy it is to perform end runs around the system. Similarly Monique Landry, a Cabinet minister in the

Mulroney government, recounted how the Canada-Quebec tug-of-war meant that when a group could not get its proposed cultural facility or athletic centre supported by one level of government, it usually found the other level only too willing to do so.

Lobbying is not scrutinized, so its practitioners cannot be held accountable. Unlike political parties, lobbyists aim to influence the behaviour of governments, elected representatives, civil servants and public officials without seeking *formal* control of the government. In 1993 when I was a member of a parliamentary committee reviewing the effectiveness of the Lobbyist Registration Act, one of the witnesses appearing before us was Harry Near. He rather typified the party official or organizer who parlays his excellent political connections and reputation into a career as a highly successful lobbyist. In his opening statement Mr. Near asserted, "Lobbyists have become part of government." This is not only an accurate observation; it is precisely the problem. Those who oppose privileged access to power and challenge the entitlements lobbyists sell are, naturally enough, dismissed by these effective and smooth-talking persuaders. Lobbyists resist any efforts to bring their activity up to the same level of public accountability that applies to every other part of government — ministers, members of Parliament, public servants — under institutional scrutiny, conflict-of-interest rules and disclosure requirements. Even the most recent amendments to the Lobbyist Registration Act, involving a role for the Ethics Commission, do not make this process any more public than it has been.

Lobbyists operate within the system and live off it. It is not just that they are political insiders, but also that they are in a parasitic relationship with the Canadian political system, able to reap the benefits of working within the system while being free from the limitations of its rules for accountability to the public. It is not the unemployed coal miner from Cape Breton or the laid-off factory worker in Owen Sound who goes to Ottawa to hang out a professional shingle as a "Government Relations Consultant" (a.k.a. "Lobbyist for Hire"). Not at all. Lobbyists are established members of Canada's political sector. They are people who, regardless of party affiliation or individual background, have spent enough time in the relatively small world of Canadian policy making and political organization to become not just well known to one another, but also increasingly alike in behaviour and general orientation. Because Ottawa is one of the world's smaller capitals, those who inhabit it are relatively few in number, their lives and careers closely intertwined. The longer one lives in Canada, and the further one advances into public life, the more one comes to understand just how small our country's governing class really is, how incestuous the relationships often are. Its membership is not, of course, confined to the city limits of the capital, but exists as a network across the country. Members of this class become familiar with one another over years and even decades of participation in Canada's endless cycle of conferences, royal commissions, task forces, parliamentary committees, constitutional forums, elections, media panels and public-policy forums, where they often make appearances as commentators and experts, helping interpret the issues and construct both the framework and content of Canada's public agenda.

Lobbyists can contribute to the system and can benefit individuals. Yet lobbyists feed off this system, and what they exact is not simply personal reward or financial gain, but also continued preferential access to the political system. The cost Canada pays for this situation is decreased governmental accountability.

After a while all the faces of those interacting with government begin to look familiar; mannerisms, outlooks and vocabulary blend together. The personalities of Canadian political life become a co-opted and socialized amalgam. Sooner or later most have connections with the multimillion-dollar lobbying business, either directly or indirectly. The Ottawa-based lobbying business includes 3,000 registered lobbyists and thousands of others, especially lawyers, who are trained in persuasively presenting information and interpreting facts before decision makers for the benefit of their clients. Lawyers are so good at this task, in fact, that they successfully lobbied the law makers to exclude the legal profession from the definition of lobbyists who must be registered! Groups and organizations who do not do their own lobbying hire these specialists — the individuals and firms that have become "a part of government" itself.

Where does this bring us in terms of accountability? The impact of these lobbying efforts can be measured each year when the finance minister presents the budget, the annual scorecard of who has succeeded in registering their points politically, and by how much. On budget day, ever watchful of their interests, representatives of lobbying and special-interest groups wait outside the Commons seeking a few seconds in front of the TV cameras to critique the finance minister's announcements. Invariably these comments reflect a highly particular perspective.

Who speaks for the whole? Presumably the government does. Yet how well can government perform this role, made up as it is of spending ministers locked in a relationship of mutual interdependency with their client constituencies?

For answers to these questions we have to go deeper still into this relationship between interest groups and the bureaucracy. We need to examine larger issues too, such as why Parliament has grown impotent in its crucial role of financial accountability, and why nobody even wants to talk about this. In 2002 when the auditor general was about to announce her findings after auditing several scandalous contracts, opposition leaders — prematurely issuing urgent statements of condemnation even days before Fraser had made her own release — sought a police investigation, then a commission of inquiry. Oddly, they never even hinted that Parliament could, or should, do the job itself.

Self-government, whether in parliamentary or personal form, means we have an obligation to see that what we realistically need for ourselves is factored into policy decisions and government spending commitments, and lobbying may be one way that citizens can articulate to government what they need. Yet responsible self-government also suggests an openness in the conduct of the public business that touches our lives collectively as citizens. In a democratic society where all citizens are guaranteed legal equality, we might well expect decisions to be openly arrived at. Certainly the rhetoric of "government of the people, by the people and for the people" sets a performance standard for elected representatives; but it also implies that the parliamentary institutions created for the express purpose of responsible government would be, if not central to this process, certainly not marginal to it either. Yet the reality is that those who daily and directly influence the course of our government do so out of the public eye, most of the time circumventing Parliament.

A citizen can rightly ask, "What happens to accountability when public business is carried on in private?" How ethical can government be in the absence of accountability? Certainly a citizen is right to ask a couple of probing questions the next time someone is heard promoting a measure in the public interest! Indeed, the persistent problems of accountability associated with the unseen operation of lobbying are connected to the unseen forces of privilege and inertia which maintain the political status quo despite demands for change. It is to these unquantifiable but very real pressures that we now turn.

6. Resistance to Change

How Privilege and Inertia Hold Accountability at Bay

In Canada the results and impacts of government programs often seem barely connected to their stated original purpose. One reason for this lack of connection is the way Canadians look at things; we seem inordinately incapable of viewing our future in our past. Something is missing that prevents us from snapping out of this dazed way of governing ourselves. We appear to be oblivious to consequences, unable to see or correct for unintended outcomes, living as if our human society and our public institutions operated in a chaotic void consisting only of a series of disconnected episodes, when of course they do not. Even things that appear random are connected; one thing leads to another. Holistic views of society help us to see this truth, whereas fragmented and reductionist analyses — for example, in the way our newspapers, periodicals, television programs and academic programs are segregated, streamed and structured — prevail in contemporary society, just as they do in Canadian government itself. They help get the job done by dividing the tasks and assist in advancing research by classifying reality into identifiable components — but there comes a tradeoff point where fragmentation and subdivided structures preclude accountability and thereby prevent real progress.

Many in government have neither knowledge of nor interest in our history. Even many MPs have little memory of Canadian parliamentary issues. This is partly due to the turnover rate for elected officials being quite high, and partly because most MPs staff their offices with young, inexperienced people keen to advance their own political careers but short on background and seasoning. A similar shallowness of vision is frequently found on the civil services side of government. In the late 1970s Ottawa began to fast-track people of talent through the civil service, rotating them frequently to ever-higher positions of responsibility. In 1983 Prime Minister Trudeau appointed me executive director of the Federal Task Force on Conflict of Interest, a position that enabled me to privately encounter many senior officials and observe up close a number of younger civil servants on the rise. Their eyes were all fixed on tomorrow. If there was a longer perspective, it was only to the horizon ahead. Few had much sense of the past, nor even, it seemed, much interest in travelling with the benefit of a rear-view mirror. The "critical paths" and "strategic plans" of their enthusiastic devising only ran, like their anticipated careers, forward into the future. I also discovered that the senior people in government had little mastery even of what was contemporaneously happening in their departments: this was the reality which flowed from too frequent shuffles of deputy ministers and Cabinet ministers. Add to this picture the fact that, as I encountered a couple of years later as an MP, many people who advocated reforms (often for fundamental changes in institutions and established practices) had neither understanding of nor interest in how we got to the present impasse they so ardently wished to escape.

It may be our Canadian curse to live simultaneously inside a culture that celebrates newness and under political institutions whose denizens propose or oppose changes and reforms often without really understanding why — except to serve their own immediate political careers. We as citizens are at least entitled to take a larger perspective and evaluate just how well we are being served by this configuration. One core truth every *successful* reformer has always grasped is that you have to start by understanding what is wrong. Action taken based on misleading concepts can be counterproductive. Even if we don't act but just pause for a bit to think about things — as counselled by those who write "wisdom" books and conduct self-help seminars — we are rendered acutely vulnerable if, as we do so, we employ concepts which are inappropriate to our reality.

Nevertheless, despite the efforts of such reformers, or perhaps ironically because of them, Canadian government is characterized by a systemic inertia. The dead weight of the existing order keeps things pinned down as they are, or reverts to the way they've always been after a quick fix has been toyed with at some superficial level. This inertia is reinforced by both established economic interests and familiar social behaviours, formed over time and now clustered around the institutions and structures that exist in the present. We can observe this in society in general and in government in particular. People seldom risk changing what serves them well, especially if nobody has yet demonstrated to them that what appears beneficial is in reality a threat or danger to their security. Unless people can clearly see that their action — or inaction — will have negative consequences, they will not feel compelled to respond differently. Defending the status quo may thus be rational, even though it is mindless. This is what makes reactionaries so powerful. They are driven by a visceral instinct for personal protection combined with a belief that they are right. Filip Palda, a professor of public administration at L'École Nationale d'Administration Publique in Hull, Quebec, who studies economic and social attitudes about government spending, suggested that one of the primary reasons government has been allowed to overspend on programs by so much for so long is that Canadians — whether politician, bureaucrat or ordinary citizen — do not appreciate the negative repercussions of most decisions:

> What they don't see directly, and something they mightn't feel so good about if they understood it, is that this money is being sucked away from another productive part of the economy ... it's easy to feel righteous and feel good in this system because it's so big and so complicated now that we can't understand the full consequences of our actions.

Canada has many people who find genuine comfort in the status quo. Those who embrace things as they stand can be found both in government and in the public at large. This is why change is resisted, why long-term detrimental effects are secondary to present tangible benefits, why reform is swatted away like a mosquito. It's also why we have so many government projects that go whimsically and expensively astray. Our vast, intricate, self-governing operation not only lacks corrective mechanisms, but, even worse, we have no capacity to see or understand this. Like recidivist prisoners who have yielded to the power and patterns of the prison system, we're "OK" within the unseen walls of our box.

New Zealand's former finance minister, Sir Roger Douglas, confronted such problems not by choice but by necessity when his country's economy hit the rocks in the mid-1980s. When interviewed by researchers from the *underground royal commission*, he made two telling points that travel well to our Canadian context. First, Douglas found that some "icon" institutions of New Zealand's welfare state had transformed over time so greatly that they not only no longer served their stated objectives, but were counterproductive to them. Measures that worked in the 1930s to alleviate suffering had a half-century later become new configurations of privilege. He added that he thought earlier generations of social activists and reformers (such as his own grandfather who, like him, had been a social democrat in office) would be aghast to come back and find their grandchildren still clinging to programs that were created to fit a short-term need during the Depression. Entitlements from these programs over the decades had created a costly and false dependency right into present times. For the many still privileged enough to be direct beneficiaries, there was very real incentive to fight to preserve these programs, to high-mindedly maintain the status quo in the name of social justice and socialism.

Douglas's second observation, relating to inertia, privilege, reform and accountability, was that once a public goal is agreed upon, the way to reach it is by lining up incentives to get there. In New Zealand's case many programs — from the ineffective way the state-owned airline was run to the artificially high market prices for certain animals due to agricultural support payments — seemed to divert people and practice *away* from the goal that in theory was in view. This idea that it is vital to line up incentives to motivate us *toward* the accomplishment of our stated purpose also helps us to recognize what is preventing us from getting there, what elements are acting as a disincentive or barrier to achieving that objective. Armed with this concept about aligning goals with incentives to reach them, we can comb through the policies and programs of our various systems — health-care, education, welfare, transportation, criminal justice — to see if they are serving as incentives or disincentives to reaching our current goals and future aspirations.

Both keeping an eye on the passage of time and its power to transform people's economic interests and social needs (along with the government's perception of them) and keeping an eye on incentives and how they can alter the speed and direction we take to reach a goal can help us achieve greater governmental accountability in the larger sense. Yet knowing where the barriers and disincentives are does not automatically mean they will be removed. A citizen might reasonably expect that when a problem has been detected in government a reform will be carried through to rectify the matter. In Canada this does not happen because of a blunt reality: resistance to change.

During the first months after the Mulroney government was formed in late 1984, the Task Force on Program Review (also known as the Nielsen Task Force, after Eric Nielsen who was responsible for it as deputy prime minister) conducted a sweeping review of the Government of Canada's operations. The task force was to figure out how and where government programs could be rationalized, or privatized, and how spending could be brought in line to curb the staggering annual deficits. A major enterprise, it brought about only limited results.

Peter Meyboom, an advisor on the task force, came to the conclusion that there was no way to reconcile politics, economics and fiscal policy, making it difficult for government to implement any real changes. He'd discovered, for example, that political forces in Quebec surrounding the dairy farmers' lobby were too powerful to allow change when the task force suggested cutting milk subsidies. Meyboom became disillusioned by the lack of impact the task force recommendations had. He felt Canadians had lost all understanding of the value of money. The result, he summarized in his report, was a general lack of concern for long-term fiscal problems.

Rather than tackling financial problems head-on while they are still manageable, government, and Canadians in general, have opted to ignore problems and let them worsen, leaving future generations to pay the price. The mismanagement of the Canada Pension Plan has been a prime example. Personal income and financial security are near the top of every Canadian's imperatives, and over the years strong public interest pushed government in various ways to create programs, such as the

CPP, that would provide financial payments to citizens as substitutes for income earned in the workplace. Yet because these programs involved so much money for so many recipients, they imposed enormous long-term financial commitments on the government — commitments that Ottawa would eventually not have the ability to meet.

This issue was of particular relevance to the young researchers of the *underground royal commission* since their generation has been left to shoulder the burden of Canada's public debt, including that generated by the Canada Pension Plan. By the time they are eligible for a pension they will likely receive only a fraction of what their parents and grandparents did. As David Slater, a former chairman of the Economic Council of Canada and general director of the Department of Finance, explained, "The Canada Pension Plan was always intended to be a partly funded and mainly a pay-as-you-go plan, that is, the people who are getting the benefits now are being paid by those who are younger and making the contributions." The number of older people, however, is increasing much more rapidly than those of working age, which means financial outlays from government for these pensions are growing much faster than the contributions are coming in. "As a result, the actual funds in the plan will be exhausted rather soon," asserted Slater. "In addition, the amount of contributions people will have to make will be greatly increased. That's the problem with a deliberately unfunded pension plan."

When Slater said "deliberately" he was referring to the clear, long-term choice government made when the CPP was set up. Specifically, the government had to decide whether pension plans would be "funded" — meaning it would collect enough revenues early in the plan's life to build up a big investment pot that could be used to meet benefits later on. This decision was significant in terms of accountability. As Slater explained, "The choice was made not to do that, but to have each generation's benefits paid for by the people who were still working." Today it may seem a rather self-indulgent exercise of power, but those in office at the time felt they had it coming to them after the deprivations of the Depression and sacrifices of the war. It also seemed, in that era of a booming economy, that the availability of money in the future would not be an issue.

Within little more than a decade, however, the danger signs began to appear. It was already time for a course correction. Between 1978 and 1981 a series of studies of Canada's retirement-income system universally agreed that there would have to be an increase in the contribution rates. "Yet the government's response was to do nothing," recalled Slater. Not even modest increases in contributions were mandated, even though such action would have made a bigger investment fund to cushion the increases in costs that were by now foreseen. The reason government did not respond was that nothing forced it to. The governing of the pension system was a symptom of the common, large-scale problem that lies behind the functioning of government in our country — the absence of accountability combined with the force of inertia. Running as vast an operation as the Canadian government in an irresponsible fashion is a great formula for generating really big problems. Slater saw this picture emerging: "What you're going to find, if you want to look at this as an investment, is that whereas for a person like myself, I probably had a 20 or 25 percent rate of return; [younger generations] may get two or three percent. It's that kind of difference."

When asked what dangers lay in the lack of accountability demonstrated by these decisions about benefits, Slater was unequivocal:

> The fundamental danger is a real intergenerational conflict. Young people today say, "We have ahead of us the prospect of paying huge increases in contributions without getting comparable improvements in our benefits. We're just going to be footing the bill for the older people. We are indeed getting a very bad deal in terms of the pay-in we make and the benefits that we're going to get."

Yet to the young members of the *underground royal commission*, it looked like nothing could upset the weight of privilege. One of the researchers, Paul Kemp, attended a government hearing in Toronto on the future of the Canada Pension Plan and discovered that he was the only person there under age 50. "Those present were all the usual lobbyists," Kemp reported, "defending the system as it was." Indeed, little has changed to the benefits structure of the CPP or who is entitled to these benefits. CPP payroll taxes were increased, starting in 1998, as the result of changes introduced by Finance Minister Paul Martin and will rise by five times until 2015 to cover these direct and increasing costs. These are modifications. The greatest burden is still on the rising generation of younger working people in Canada.

Ottawa yields endless such stories about resistance to change. This is not astonishing since politics itself is largely a dance where some propose change and others resist it. That's what Parliament, the dance floor of democracy, is all about. Yet here again there is something deeper we should look at if we want to seriously understand *why* our government is often so shockingly unaccountable. We need to see beyond political resistance to change, the kind we get from *individual* reactionaries and vested interests, to something quite different: *institutional* resistance to change.

Bob Couchman, for decades one of Canada's most pioneering of social workers, witnessed first hand the transfer of social responsibility from families and individuals to the state. He saw how "the new welfare-state culture of Canada seemed to be substituting trained professionals for neighbours, friends and family." The shift from informal and spontaneous support systems "was being justified on the basis that too many people had fallen through the gaps of the traditional system." The governmental response was "a universal social safety net run by well-trained professionals to ensure the social well-being of all citizens." The consequence of professionalizing and regulating care-giving systems "served to promote dependency on the part of many families." That set the stage.

Next came the evidence that this elaborate and costly social-service structure was set up and functioning in ways that served its own ends more than the needs of those it ostensibly existed to help. Trying to understand why, Couchman found that one of the fundamental causes turned out to be the fact that it operated in the absence of any sort of comprehensive or integrating accountability. The evidence appeared in what Couchman calls "the silo effect." This was perhaps the inevitable result of a governmental approach to social welfare; government is organized in Canada on a line-department basis, even though in reality the world and its issues don't line up in neat columns according to departmental structures. The peculiar kind of "accountability" which results from this is by the system to the system, not by the system to the citizen or the citizen's elected representative. A particular government department may achieve full reporting and financial accountability up and down its own hierarchical structure for an individual program yet still be unaccountable within the system as a whole or to the citizen. Because each department operated like a separate silo, the attack on Canada's social problems lacked overall coherence and ultimate accountability.

As Couchman began working with the bureaucracy of the social-welfare system, he gained a rare overview of how the community, government services, professional elites and institutions functioned. He was struck by "the incredible effort required to bring simple, rational order to human elements which are complex, emotionally charged, often ugly, and very much interrelated to one another." The administrative system, however, took these people and neighbourhood cultures and divided their needs into health, education, recreation and social requirements. Professionals would then be trained to address each *separate* need using a language specific to their discipline. Recalled Couchman:

> I was suddenly jolted into recognizing this phenomenon at one of those classic case conferences which were so popular among professionals in the 1960s. Ten individuals representing education, mental health, child welfare, corrections and the welfare department had been called together for a two-hour conference to discuss John, a 10-year-old boy, and his family of six. Due to the seriousness of the child's difficulties, several agencies sent a supervisor, in addition to a social worker or teacher. After the initial round of introductions we soon became aware that each agency was investing between four and 140 hours a month working with John and his family. Despite this effort he was steadily deteriorating.

At a critical juncture in this particular meeting, with all its complex discussion on what was really wrong with John and who was doing what about it, Couchman heard Ned McKeown of the Toronto Board of Education announce in extreme frustration that for half the funds being spent on John and his family, he could provide the boy with his own exclusive special-education teacher and assign a full-time trained homemaker to the family. "Everyone knew Ned was correct," admitted Couchman, "but no one had the professional courage to challenge the system so that the right thing could be done. As a result, each of us covered ourselves in the prescribed professional manner and John's situation continued to worsen."

During his years working within Canada's social-welfare system, Bob Couchman discovered both how and why institutions resist change.[4] The approach to social issues in Canada became institutionalized as our Canadian welfare state evolved, which is why, after decades of operating programs to deal with all our social problems, we still have homeless people on the streets, people begging at the corners, an increasing number of children living in poverty and high levels of functional illiteracy. It was not just that the system had bypassed the people it had been created to help, but that when someone saw the need for a course correction and signalled its importance, no one was willing or able to make a change. Over time that engenders a defeatist attitude. Why bother even trying?

This resistance to healthy political evolution means, in turn, that the forces of inertia and privilege that have contributed to the erosion of accountability in Canada are likely to persist. The phenomenon is self-reinforcing. From regional subsidies for economically marginal activity to social programs without cost projections — it appears we are prepared to continue *repeated* failures. Government in Ottawa set aside the very reports it had commissioned on future funding for the Canada Pension Plan in the 1970s, deliberately refused to heed urgent warnings about the debt spiral and compounding interest, willingly distorted the Constitution by using its unrestricted spending power to expand into provincial jurisdiction. Time and again the Government of Canada overrode Quebec's valid and urgently expressed concern to maintain constitutional integrity, fostering a strong separatist movement that now threatens the country's future. Why did our ability to see cause and effect disappear? A significant part of the answer lies in the fact that, having gained responsible government, where the elected representatives could raise issues, consider ideas and hold the government of the day to account, we allowed it to slip away. Those who wielded power were not uncomfortable to silently witness and sometimes contribute to Parliament's erosion as our national political institution for accountability.

7. Responsible Government Won and Lost

Parliamentarians Play-Act Their Accountability Roles

Getting to Parliament, newly elected MPs are often shocked to find that *on a functional level* we do not have responsible government. Before I was first elected in 1984 I'd spent years training and preparing to participate in an accountable parliamentary process as the representative of the 100,000 citizens in my district, but I discovered there simply were no effective means by which to do so. My experience was no aberration. For most MPs, getting to Parliament Hill is like going to play hockey in an arena but finding no ice to skate on. In recent decades many MPs on both sides of the House have given vent, often in acute frustration and occasionally with considerable eloquence, to this sense of futility. It's even a bit ominous because the historical conditions that first gave rise to responsible government in Canada seem so familiar in our present circumstances. You start to wonder if history doesn't repeat itself.

Consider, for example, that in the early 1800s government was run by a small group of the powerful and privileged, or what is called an oligarchy. As confident in their own plans as they were arrogant in their use of power, these colonial leaders paid little heed to elected representatives in the legislature, and didn't really need to. By about 1815 demands for reform began to build. By the 1830s our expanding Loyalist colonies of British North America, increasingly outgrowing the forms of overseas government laid down at the close of the American Revolution, were growing less content to be ruled from above by a local oligarchy. As grievances piled up, reform movements developed. More people began expressing an impatient desire to gain local control over local affairs.

The British government in London neglected this pressure. The oligarchy gave only token attention to petitions, resolutions, practical grievances and real problems. (Is the picture looking familiar?) For its part the government seemed focused instead on its international trade agenda. The economy was globalizing. Britain's rise as an industrial power meant the world wanted its manufactured products, not just access to its colonial markets controlled under the older mercantilist trading system. After the American Revolution the remnant British North American colonies were being marginalized, losing their relative importance in the new patterns of world trade. In matters of governance the creaking colonial system continued to operate almost as a matter of habit, and Britain was largely content to keep things as they were, which meant supporting an increasingly unpopular political system. (Does this not seem to be echoing across the years too?)

The parallels don't end there. Back then the colonial assemblies represented the people but did not fully control either law making or public finances, and reformers felt these important roles should be taken up more rigorously and responsibly; they even wrote about the absence of accountability in publications of the day. Some main sources of government revenue were not under the control of elected representatives. Their enacted laws were often revised by the Cabinet ministers, vetoed by the governor or set aside for consideration by the overseas imperial authorities. Government was not responsible — or accountable — to the elected assemblies, and the constituency representatives complained, then as today, about being as impotent as the people they represented.

Real power lay in the hands of the small governing executive, an oligarchy in each colonial province — called, for example, the "Council of

Twelve" in Nova Scotia, the "Chateau Clique" in Quebec and the "Family Compact" in Ontario. The situation was not dissimilar in other British North American colonies such as Newfoundland, Prince Edward Island, Vancouver Island and British Columbia. Each colony faced particular issues and unique grievances, but sooner or later all roads led back to the same central problem of the unaccountable exercise of power by those in positions of privilege. Elected members in the legislative assemblies, weak against the inertia of a solidly planted establishment, expressed frustration over being ineffectual and sought to expose the hollowness of these nominal institutions of representative democracy. As decades passed it grew clearer that little could be achieved to respond to people's needs until these self-reinforcing oligarchies had been dislodged, or at least made to govern in some accountable fashion. The battle to gain responsible government was under way.

In Nova Scotia, Quebec (Canada East) and Ontario (Canada West) moderate reform parties emerged under strong leaders such as Joseph Howe, Louis Lafontaine and Robert Baldwin, pushing politically for responsible government. Others, such as Louis-Joseph Papineau and William Lyon Mackenzie, sought swifter changes to the shortcomings and abuses of the existing system, leading armed rebellions in 1837 to overthrow the oligarchy by force. After British soldiers suppressed this Canadian revolution-in-the-making, Lord Durham was quickly dispatched from Home Office in London to figure out what the devil was wrong in the colonies.

Given that ministers in government were not paying much attention to the people's elected representatives in the legislature, Durham recommended making them live together under one roof. Then they'd be forced to talk together, listen, debate, answer, argue and explain. There were to be other benefits to Durham's forced marriage of Cabinet and legislature. Elected representatives could no longer just give fiery speeches atop a country stump or in a village hall, or to one another in the echoing legislative chamber, but would now have to address their sharp complaints directly to those wielding power. Ministers of the Crown, by the same token, could no longer make decisions or set policies without facing directly those who might criticize and even improve them. Moreover, by imposing a new rule that ministers themselves had to be chosen from among the members of the legislature, ministers and members would now share a common footing;

they would moderate one another, a process that institutionalized accountability and ensured more focused responsibility in providing peace, order and good government.

By 1848, with Durham's proposal implemented in a new Constitution enacted by Britain's Parliament, responsible government was in full swing in Canada East, Canada West and Nova Scotia. Within the decade it had also been gained by Britain's other eastern colonies: Prince Edward Island, New Brunswick and Newfoundland. This plan for responsible government was carried forward into the new Canadian Constitution in 1867. Other provinces that subsequently joined Confederation operated on the same plan.

The theory of responsible government is one thing; the present-day operation of government in Canada, quite another. It would be overly dramatic to say that responsible government in Canada has collapsed, but there is very little remaining to actually support it. To come to grips with the absence of accountability in the way Parliament works, not in theory but in practice, it is instructive to begin with some of the myths, fictions and misconceptions pertaining to governing doctrines. Perhaps four of the greatest myths are the following:

Myth #1: Accountability is enhanced because power is divided between different levels of government.

Myth #2: The re-election of a government shows that people endorse it.

Myth #3: MPs go to Ottawa to run the country.

Myth #4: General elections give the winning party a mandate to govern.

Let's consider each in turn to see how our actual government system has become shrouded behind these misconceptions and myths.

Myth #1: Accountability is enhanced because power is divided between different levels of government.

Jurisdictional clarity, which is a precondition for accountability, and which is represented in our Constitution by the division of powers between the national and provincial governments, no longer exists in Canada today.

As we saw in the case of the Canada Infrastructure Works Program discussed in Chapter 3 — not to mention in the more challenging areas of health, transportation, security, environment, trade, labour and social services — when it comes to figuring out who is responsible for government spending, the buck stops nowhere; the result is that *accountability is impossible.* Over time, combining a parliamentary system with our federal system, which formally has two levels of government (national and provincial) and operationally has three (national, provincial and local), actually fragmented jurisdictional accountability, to the point where it has been lost completely. Seldom in all my years around government did I find anyone who said, "I did that. I'm the one responsible." Instead it was invariably, "I'll have to consult my advisors on this." When it comes to the way our government works today, no one really knows who is doing what, or who is responsible.

Myth #2: The re-election of a government shows that people endorse it.

The Canadian electoral system does not accurately measure voter support. Winning an election does not mean that a party is supported by a majority of the population; nor can the victory be cited as evidence that the public approves of the party's style of governing.

Our electoral system is dysfunctional in terms of its ability to translate levels of popular support for different parties across the country into a comparable ratio of seats in Parliament. Because the system was designed to determine elections fought between only two parties, it has been out of date since the 1920s when the country moved from a two-party to a multiparty system. Yet privilege and inertia have kept this defective system in place, which is just one more reason why many Canadians are increasingly disowning the electoral process and the distorted results it generates.

Our country does not speak with one voice, but is divided into some 300 constituencies. Within these constituencies, or ridings, those who are elected often assume office with only a plurality, not a majority, of the votes cast by people living there. A plurality just means getting more votes than any other candidate, which is all it takes to win. Typically, four, five or even six candidates run in each riding. The result is that many MPs go to Ottawa with only a minority of voters having cast ballots for them. For example, when I was elected to Parliament in 1984, it was with 44 percent of the popular vote; when I was re-elected in 1988, it was again with 44 percent of the popular vote; when I was defeated in 1993, it was still with a mid-40s mark of popular vote. Whether I won — or lost — depended not on the accuracy of a representative electoral system, but on the relative fates and fortunes of the numerous other candidates also in the field. Although the majority of voters in my riding of Etobicoke–Lakeshore did not vote for me, there I was in Parliament, voting for the GST, for borrowing bills, for free trade, for Meech Lake. When I looked around the Commons at the 294 other elected "representatives," I saw a number of MPs from all parties who won with considerably narrower victories and even lower pluralities than mine.

The second Chrétien Liberal government, with its "huge majority" of seats in the Commons, took office having won only 38 percent of the popular vote. In 2000 Jean Chrétien and the Liberals won their third majority in a row, with the support of a minority of the electorate — 42 percent of the popular vote. Nevertheless, the Liberals secured 172 of the 301 seats in the Commons, or 57 percent of the seats. Holding a majority of seats gives the *appearance* of a majority government because of the distorting hall-of-mirrors effect of our antiquated (though much tinkered with) electoral system. The reality, however, is that the levels of *representation* in our national legislative assembly are not an accurate reflection of the levels of voter support, of citizens' considered electoral conclusions.

So once again we discover that we do not have "representative government" in Canada and that our political superstructure, along with the laws and institutions it brings into being, rests upon shaky supports.

Myth #3: MPs go to Ottawa to run the country.

It is *not* Parliament's role to run the country. That's what the government does.

In the overall structure of Canadian government, the primary role of Parliament is to provide accountability in the way government is being run. If people (including MPs) don't know what government is really doing, it is a measure of how greatly Parliament has failed to shed light on the proper object of its attention.

Unfortunately there is confusion here because many people *think* that Parliament is the government. Even many MPs think and act this way with embarrassing frequency. The bleak truth about the role of MPs in Canada is that — and I'm speaking as someone who once was one — their main task ends the very night they are elected. That's when their aggregated numbers determine which party, and which small group within that party, will form the government. Having then served their leadership-selection function, MPs are kept busy and generally out of trouble for several years with highly public make-work projects until it's time for the party's leaders to again work MPs up into a state of partisan fervour sufficient, the leaders hope, to win another election.

Perhaps the distinction between the government and Parliament can best be illustrated by comparing Cabinet ministers in Parliament to a hand in a glove. The fact that one fits inside the other, so that they move as one and even function together, does not mean they are the same thing. Because our MPs and government leaders (the prime minister and Cabinet ministers) are combined institutionally within the legislative assembly, the hand is in the glove. This reality, and the appearance of it, contributes to the confusion of roles. It is the government that runs the country, and it is the job of Parliament to hold that government to account. Today, however, Parliament is failing to perform its primary role. Parliament, in fact, is no longer an institution of representative democracy, but has instead become a *government institution*. The elected representatives of the people do not hold the government to account, but rather function as extensions of the government itself, and generally are satisfied and proud to do so. Canadian legislatures do perform important roles in recruitment and education, for it is through the legislative chamber that new people are constantly drawn into government service, and it is also from MPs that a stream of publications, speeches and public-service advertisements flows to the public. Yet neither of these functions has much to do with holding government accountable. They are, if anything, just the opposite: a measure of how far and in how many ways our national legislature has devolved into little more than an operating extension of government — its recruitment office and public relations bureau.

Some political scientists add that Parliament performs a legitimizing role. By this they mean that when the government has decided to do something, it may appear more acceptable to the country or to the international community if Parliament enacts a law or passes a resolution endorsing it. Legitimacy is extremely important for a government because if the people (and the governments of other countries) believe someone is legitimately in power, or is acting with the endorsement of the country's principal democratic institution, they will obey even if they don't agree. Again, however, according legitimacy to a government is in many important respects the very antithesis of holding it accountable.

Myth #4: General elections give the winning party a mandate to govern.

The "mandate theory," even in the best of circumstances, was never more than a convenient constitutional fiction.

Powerful governments have long promoted a doctrine of parliamentary democracy which holds that once elected by virtue of winning the most seats in a general election, regardless of the size of the party's popular vote, the government has a mandate to deal with any issue that comes up during the life of that Parliament. Most political scientists and media commentators also operate within this accepted view and have, along with many compliant politicians, reinforced its popularity by their teachings, commentaries and behaviour. This doctrine makes sense as a practical approach to the many details and issues that can never be aired and debated, let alone anticipated, in an election campaign. It nevertheless enshrines a very bold fiction in a country that operates on the theory of being a representative parliamentary democracy; it is one of the major reasons why Canadian governments have lost credibility and Canadian legislatures are generally viewed with disrespect, even by many who are members of them.

To assert that a government can go to war, amend the country's constitution or reverse a whole pattern of trade policies or immigration programs without ever talking about such courses of action in its election campaign is to stretch the mandate doctrine further than is reasonable in a parliamentary democracy. Yet each of these has happened in Canada. To brazenly reverse aspects of the mandate — clear promises made by the political party that won voters' endorsement during the campaign — such as freezing prices and wages (as Prime Minister Trudeau did, although he'd pledged he wouldn't) or cancelling the acquisition of nuclear-powered submarines (as Prime Minister Mulroney did, even though he'd said his government would buy them) or continuing the GST and the free trade treaty (as Prime Minister Chrétien has, despite ardently campaigning against both) stretches the doctrine to the point of meaninglessness, and, not surprisingly, the government loses its authority and legitimacy. If prime ministers shrug with indifference, so will citizens.

People reasonably understand that some issues not addressed in an election campaign may later emerge and influence the stated positions of the party in office. Most Canadians also accept that the government basically governs as it must, and even as it chooses, provided it can maintain majority support in the Commons. The mandate doctrine itself, however, is increasingly untenable. Many Canadians are now prepared to challenge it by declaring that a mandate does *not* empower a government to deal with any and all issues or crises that arise over its term in office, especially if those issues were never discussed in the previous election campaign. All political parties campaign on the basis of some program; the party that forms the government may even try to implement part of it! Yet many Canadians have grown increasingly skeptical about the election promises of parties right across the political spectrum, based on practice and performance. Part of the reason for this shift is that we understand an election is no longer principally an accountability session. Elements of renewal and accountability assuredly remain part of an election, but only a part.

To reveal the different ways a majority government mandate can cover vastly different practices and policies, just contrast the two Liberal majority governments, both headed by Pierre Trudeau, elected in 1974 and 1980. When the Liberals won a convincing majority in the 1974 general election, we saw how the parliamentary theories about an electoral mandate camouflaged the actual practices of the government that had received the public's "blank cheque" to govern. Prime Minister Trudeau, suggests Richard Gwyn in his biography of him, "interpreted a majority victory as a mandate to goof off."[5] When the Conservatives, led by Joe Clark, defeated the Liberals in May 1979, Marc Lalonde, a principal minister in the Trudeau Cabinet, looked back bleakly and saw no significant achievement of his government in many portfolios, especially the economic ones. "It was quite clear in our minds that if we came back, it would have to mean something," Lalonde later explained in a 1982 interview.[6]

Back in power following the 1980 election, the Liberals displayed a newfound conviction, according to authors Robert Sheppard and Michael Valpy, that Ottawa "must reassert itself in a number of key fields — energy, regional economic development, fiscal transfers and constitutional reform." The revived Trudeau government soon "embarked on a new age of confrontational politics — competitive rather than co-operative federalism."[7] In the spring of 1980, the same writers said, Pierre Trudeau was "probably wielding more raw prime ministerial power than any of his predecessors. He had a majority government and was facing a dispirited opposition ... his caucus and party were beholden to him for leading them out of the wilderness; and ... his few promises in the winter campaign effectively gave him a free hand to pursue the national interest in his own fashion."[8]

This gap between what leaders say during campaigns and then do in office is not a uniquely Liberal phenomenon. After the Progressive Conservatives won a huge majority government in 1984, Prime Minister Mulroney used his "licence to govern" to initiate a free trade treaty with the United States, thereby reversing the historic position of the Conservative Party and his own position during his successful PC leadership campaign, when he had made specific statements opposing "continentalism." His government soon began to get into real trouble on this issue, "not because they had promised more than they had delivered," observed pollster and author Michael Adams, "but because they had delivered more than they had promised, namely the free trade agreement with the United States."[9] Free trade, which had not been mentioned during the 1984 election campaign and thus could not in any sense be considered part of the people's mandate given to the Mulroney Conservatives, consequently became the central issue of the 1988 election campaign.

These important policy reversals by Liberal and Progressive Conservative governments show how, at a theoretical and policy level, the ballot box is not necessarily an effective mechanism for ensuring accountability — at least not if one examines the correlation between election campaign promises and subsequent government actions. This flip-flop approach has become endemic in recent decades — on such matters as new military helicopters, repeal of the GST and renegotiation of the free trade treaty — a discrepancy between promise and performance that cannot be ignored as a factor contributing to the decline in the credibility of our political leaders and a growing embarrassment about our governmental processes.

These four political myths or constitutional fictions are no longer believable in the face of the reality of Parliament's structural operations and performance record. Parliament has lost credibility and relevance not only among most Canadians, but also with senior civil servants and many highly frustrated MPs. Parliament has turned into a scene of bittersweet theatre, sadly incapable of being accountable even unto itself. Does this have consequences for Canadians? Unfortunately, and sometimes tragically, the answer is yes. Nowhere is the increasing irrelevance of Parliament, as well as the government's tendency to ignore or overstep its mandate, more evident than in the realm of military and defence policy. The same accountability issues relevant to any area of government apply to the Canadian military too, except that the consequences of incompetence and unaccountability are more serious because "mistakes" may risk the lives of Canadians in uniform and the lives of others. Accordingly, in a system of responsible government decisions regarding the Canadian Armed Forces should call for the very highest standards of accountability.

When I was parliamentary secretary for the Department of National Defence in 1992, in Washington one morning driving with Defence Minister Marcel Masse to a meeting at the Pentagon, we learned that External Affairs Minister Barbara McDougall had announced Canada would send a further 1,200 soldiers overseas for the UN peacekeeping mission in the former Yugoslavia. We were reading faxed copies of a newspaper report. There had been no consultation, not even an inquiry to ascertain the availability of military personnel for this mission — at least none that either of us knew anything about. Certainly there had been no debate about it in Parliament, let alone a vote by Parliament to authorize and support the deployment. Similarly, during the summer of 1990 when the Iraqi forces of Saddam Hussein invaded Kuwait, Prime Minister Mulroney announced, not before the House of Commons but into a television camera, that Canadian ships, aircraft and military personnel were being dispatched to the Persian Gulf. Canadians learned the news of this major commitment as a fait accompli, a military mission overseas, undebated and unauthorized by Parliament.

The ascendancy of prime ministerial power at the expense of parliamentary accountability has transformed the country in profound ways, as these matters concerning the deployment of the Canadian Forces overseas demonstrate. Colonel (Ret) John English explained to researchers for the *underground royal commission*, "Over the years we got in this business of deploying peacekeeping forces by order-in-council or by Cabinet decision — that they will go over and there will be no parliamentary debate called. There will be no debate within the Canadian public at large." A succession of Canadian prime ministers — William Lyon Mackenzie King, John Diefenbaker, Lester Pearson, Pierre Trudeau, Brian Mulroney, Jean Chrétien — has sought to play a major role on the international stage; these leaders have appropriated for themselves through the Privy Council Office a significant role in relation to foreign policy and defence matters. "No minister likes to mess with the food on a prime minister's plate," observed John Dixon, who served as Kim Campbell's senior advisor when she was defence minister, "so he stands back to let the prime minister run foreign policy and defence. Meanwhile, the prime minister rightly thinks his minister is running the Defence Department. So there is a deep confusion that has been institutionalized in our structure of government."

This confusion has only been increased by the absence of Parliament from any decision-making or review process with respect to foreign policy and defence matters. While it is not Parliament's role to run the government, it is Parliament's job to air issues, debate different considerations, approve the annual budgets of the Defence and Foreign Affairs ministries, vote to ratify treaties and authorize military involvement overseas. So why doesn't it? The rise of "partyism" in Parliament means that our national legislature now functions more as an arena for team sport than as a centre for contending issues and serious debate on legitimate differences of policy. Party solidarity, considered a prime virtue in this setting at all times, is especially valued and enforced in times of crisis and international confrontation. The government's instinct to show solidarity with our allies in collective security arrangements when a global crisis hits is then refracted back into its control over Parliament. Why give hostility and dissent a chance to display itself on the floor of the House of Commons when we want to show unanimity and solidarity of purpose?

With respect to these fundamental military matters, Parliament no longer plays its historic and proper role, is no longer an instrument for accountability on the national political scene or touching the affairs of state. Our country's original policy was that no Canadian in uniform could ever be sent beyond our borders without parliamentary authorization. The prime minister and ministers of defence and foreign affairs would have to justify such life-and-death policies to the people's elected representatives. For some even that seemed inadequate. When debating Canadian participation in the Boer War in 1899, for example, Sir Wilfrid Laurier suggested holding a national referendum on the question. At a minimum Parliament was always fully involved in authorizing war activity. In August 1914 Prime Minister Robert Borden interrupted his Muskoka vacation to summon Parliament, which debated and voted to declare war on Germany. The Borden government had, moreover, also been on the brink of holding a national referendum on going to war, but pulled back at the last moment — a hesitation in taking the matter directly to the people that Arthur Meighen, attorney general of Canada at the time and later Conservative Party leader and prime minister, came to openly regret. In 1939 Parliament, now under the leadership of Prime Minister Mackenzie King, again voted, following debate, upon a resolution for a declaration of war. However, when Canadian forces sailed in 1950 for Korea, they did so without the approval of Parliament; the Cabinet of Prime Minister St. Laurent, dispensing with the required parliamentary debate, merely issued an order-in-council as authorization. The limp excuse that Korea was a so-called "police action" by the United Nations, not a war, was already enough to persuade some folks that Parliament did not have to be involved. Although it was not a "war," 27,000 Canadians served overseas under arms and over 800 died in the "action." From Wilfrid Laurier to Louis St. Laurent, the country had turned 180 degrees and a new pattern was set. Our prime ministers in the modern era came to think that Canadians should just trust them to do the right thing.

Thus it was Cabinet, not Parliament, that approved the decision to intervene in Somalia in October 1992. The mission was presented in the Commons during Question Period and to the media in press briefings as traditional peacekeeping, but it was not in any fashion like other United Nations military missions with which Canadians were familiar. The nature and purpose of the military's role, having been neither clarified nor endorsed by Parliament, was ambiguous and uncertain to those in the field, a situation that recurred in late 2001 and 2002 when Canadian troops were sent to Afghanistan in an cloud of uncertainty about their overall mission, and even about such matters as taking prisoners.

Our soldiers' experiences in Bosnia in the early 1990s highlight the problems encountered when accountability is avoided for long periods. Ambush greeted the Canadian soldiers who thought they had been sent on a peacekeeping mission. Hatred between different ethnic groups created deep and mean responses, and Canadians found themselves right in the middle. Even the seasoning gained from Canada's decades' long role in keeping peace between Turks and Greeks in Cyprus was no preparation for what the soldiers faced in Bosnia. Furthermore, silence on the home front covered this operation with a mask of unreality. Canadian soldiers, on the ground in a hot war, discovered no one in Ottawa was seriously accountable for what was unfolding. This examination of Parliament's role (or lack thereof) in military matters shows that the consequences of inaction, or action based on inaccurate or incomplete information, can be extremely serious. While the stakes are higher and the results of decisions more dramatic, the lack of accountability evident in both Parliament's and the government's attitude toward the Canadian Armed Forces is indicative of the way in which contemporary Canadian government operates in general.

In theory government is subject to a number of constraints. It must be accountable to an official Opposition in the House of Commons. It must enact new laws through Parliament. It is constitutionally obligated to meet Parliament every year, submit a budget and all spending estimates to Parliament annually and call a general election at least every five years. The government's laws and actions can be challenged in court and scrutinized by an independent judiciary. Provincial governments can balance Ottawa's broad power. All the while a competitive and often critical news media continually examines the government's exercise of power. Yet in reality, for every minute of reckoning achieved by Parliament, there are hours of non-accountability. For every law passed openly in Parliament, a dozen more are enacted inconspicuously by orders-in-council. For every budget item scrutinized, a thousand others are deemed approved unexamined. For every election held when the government's back is to the wall or its constitutional time limit of five years has run out, three more are self-servingly called at the moment most propitious to those who already hold power. Parliament, once central to expressing peoples' views on issues facing Canadians, has become an anachronism ever since this role was scooped out by government-hired public opinion pollsters, leaving the House of Commons a hollow chamber rather than a connector between Canadians and our government's policies and programs. Parliament's role in controlling government spending has been eviscerated, procedurally and behaviourally, step by step over the past 30 years, to the point where MPs no longer control the public purse strings either.

As citizens we no doubt conclude, the more we watch television or read newspaper accounts about the increasing role of lobbyists and interest groups and the ineffectiveness of our elected representatives, that our own chance to individually influence public decisions grows slimmer and more remote with each passing day. We do not have representative government so much as a system of government where representations are made behind closed doors and away from any mechanisms of accountability. So it's hardly a surprise that, as reported by Leger Marketing in April 2002, 69 percent of Canadians think that the federal government is corrupt. Some citizens have expressed their growing dissatisfaction with the decision making of elected and appointed officials by suggesting that government should hold community forums and town hall meetings as a regular part of the ongoing governing process. People do not advance such alternatives unless they feel dissatisfied with the existing arrangements. Those who make these suggestions are trying to improve a system evidently in need of an overhaul. Others just boycott it altogether, staying away from polling stations on election day.

The power of Parliament to monitor the government's activities and provide accountability to the Canadian people once came about through the mechanism of approving the government's spending program, voting for taxes, approving of borrowing, questioning Cabinet ministers and enacting or amending the laws that the government introduced in Parliament. Along the way there was debate, sometimes humour, and invariably deep differences of opinion. Today these parliamentary powers are exercised formally but seldom substantively. However, in considering the ephemeral nature of governmental accountability in our Canadian context, it would be wrong to focus on Parliament alone; Parliament was once our most important national political institution, but not the only one. It functions within a matrix of institutions that connect and interact. One's role picks up where another's leaves off. If Parliament no longer exercises much effective power, it is not because power has evaporated, but because it has flowed and been taken elsewhere. Each governmental institution in our capital and across the country is part of a larger picture we need to see more clearly for accurate perception of our functioning realities.

Most Canadians believe, and are in fact encouraged to think, that the MP is our connector. We believe that MPs, individually and collectively, make the system work, especially in terms of accountability. Isn't that also what we teach our children? Don't we say the meaning of responsible government — the executive held to account — is all about answering to the people's elected representatives in Parliament? The truth is, the Parliament of Canada is no longer a seriously functioning part of the accountability equation. As an MP I was no connector. I was a pushed and battered shock absorber between the needs of the people I represented and the predetermined plans of a tightly controlled top-down government. In my case it was the Mulroney government because I was elected as a Tory; had I run and been elected as a Grit, I'd have experienced the same phenomenon under the Trudeau or Chrétien governments. This is not a partisan issue; it is a parliamentary issue. Until you've been there to experience this, you cannot hope to know with just how much excruciating humiliation parliamentarians are forced to absorb and internalize our governing system's deepest contradictions — while seeking to salvage a measure of human dignity with a broken smile toward constituents and into the cameras.

During its cross-country interviews the *underground royal commission* encountered many MPs and former MPs who had similar views about their experiences in Parliament. Reg Alcock, Liberal MP for Winnipeg–South, was both perceptive and clear:

> The House actually has enormous authority, but at certain key points, who exercises that authority is controlled by one person — the prime minister. We need to separate that to allow the House to function as a body to demand accountability from the government. That's what it has to be.

In a similar way George Baker, a Newfoundland Liberal MP for some 30 years before being appointed to the Senate in 2002, pointed out that once MPs are elected to the House they face "a situation where a member has to be in good standing with the party even to get on Question Period. A member has to be in good standing with the party leader and the whip in order to even speak in the House of Commons. Where does this leave members of Parliament?" Former Conservative Cabinet minister John Crosbie was candid too. He said an MP can be "a good representative of their area but as members of a party influencing policy, what a government actually does, rather than settling up this man's unemployment claim or this woman's rent problem, they basically don't have much influence. They are a very frustrated group."

Having been in Parliament, I share the contradictory feelings of Canadians who are disenchanted with the way our country's system of government works, but are also aware of so much that is good and of permanent value in it. The problem? Our democratic theory is premised on citizens and citizens' elected representatives playing an active and informed role in the political system, but theory is not matched by opportunity. Instead, MPs and the people they represent are relegated to the periphery of political life by government officials who prefer to say, in effect, "Just trust us." In this atmosphere it's most beneficial for members to portray themselves as ombudsmen for their constituents and lean heavily toward service and problem solving and speaking up for local concerns, all helpful for getting re-elected. That's how Canadians evidently perceive them too.

For instance, a 1999 Environics poll asked respondents to rank the most important functions of MPs from a list provided. "Representing local concerns to Parliament" was chosen by 42 percent; 24 percent said it was "solving constituents' problems"; 22 percent picked "providing their constituents with information on government." Only nine percent said the fourth role, "supporting the objectives of their political party," should rank as most important. Even more revealing is that none of the "most important" roles identified in the question had anything to do with holding government accountable or scrutinizing spending. The pollsters, being realists, didn't even bother to ask. They, too, know that what we teach the children about responsible government is not the way it really works. On good days the most that happens is that MPs play-act at accountability.

With this evaluation of the institutional and behavioural problems facing those who represent the people of Canada in mind, it makes sense to now step back a little further, or rise above the parliamentary fray a little higher, and see the nature of just who we are, the Canadian citizens that our MPs endeavour to represent.

Who We Are

8. Canada

The Sponge

No line can be drawn in Canada between government and non-government responsibility any longer, if it ever could. Our modern era has seen the "private sector" and the "public sector" put into the blender. The consequence of this blending — the systemic impossibility of accountability — has had long-term implications for the country and how our political culture developed.

In this era when politicians and the political processes of the country are disparaged, often by politicians themselves, the irony is that each of us has had to become highly political, not as card-carrying partisans, but in the way government operations have become integrated into our daily decisions and orderly routines. How else can a Canadian cope in so busily governed a society as our own except by becoming highly political? The ability to deal successfully with all the branches and programs of Canadian government, and with our multiple, separate levels of government, has become for many a matter of planning, for most a matter of progressing, and for some even a matter of survival. We Canadians have never been without a strong framework of government in our lives, but that long-standing pattern has now taken new form.

Let's recap the problem: a concept used when trying to describe the general and inclusive realm of Canadian governmental affairs is the "public sector." This category is then usually juxtaposed with the term "private sector." Yet today both terms are misleading and create confusion because no line divides these two conceptual spaces from one another in our country. They are one and the same thing. Totally blended and without boundaries.

Despite privatization, and in some instances because of it — just consider the widely varying combinations of government, non-government and underground marketing systems for beer, wine and spirits across Canada as one example — we have in place a distribution and sales network that defies all known descriptions and traditional categories. Today government and business intercourse in Canada extends far beyond the realms of economics or health, across education and transportation, into security, personal finance, culture and sport. Each one of us, as a citizen, is carried along both with and within it, part and parcel of this process which defines the context of our activities and the meaning of our individual pursuits.

To be talking today about private and public sectors is as ludicrous as describing the danger of flat-earth explorers falling off the world: say what you will, believe what you want, there is no edge there! These terms, derived from earlier days and prior concepts of private property and common wealth, of corporate exclusivity and civic-minded national public service, now cloud more than clarify any perception or analysis about what really is going on in Canada. What we have is neither a public nor a private sector (nor a third or fourth or fifth sector, as some analysts have been suggesting recently) but rather a single, highly integrated sector that, by its porous and flexible quality, its ability to absorb, its capacity to hold a little or a lot and appear the same either way, to expand when pulled or contract when squeezed, resembles more than anything else ... a sponge!

The Great Canadian Sponge evolved as a result of changes in our development as a country. Building Canada required large-scale projects that often exceeded the financial and organizational resources of the country's business community. This out of necessity called for government to play a role in shaping the destiny of our people and the development of our vast natural resources. Early in the 20th century a second dimension was added to this role. Government ownership of elements of economic production and distribution was advocated in the face of rapacious practices in forestry and mining by essentially unregulated private businesses. It was in the public interest to have government own and operate certain key sectors of economic activity so that the benefits would spread directly and evenly to all, rather than be exploited for the advantage of a few. The excesses of capitalist ways had spawned a Canadian response of conservation, resource management and sharing the wealth.

Some saw these proposals as socialist ideas, but many others in Canada's main political parties considered them pragmatic policies in the face of raw greed, wasteful plundering of natural resources and the impoverishment and injury of Canadian workers. In Canada specific expression of this new thinking led to the nationalization of a number of private companies in such fields as electricity generation, telephone systems and railroads. The new ideology was principally a blend of social justice, concern for the environment, a desire for efficiency, and default. Government got stuck with picking up broken pieces and putting them together in the public interest at the public's expense, as in the case of the Canadian National Railway. The nationalization of industries was carried out largely by Conservative governments, and somewhat by Liberal ones, long before North America's first socialist government was ever elected, in Saskatchewan in 1944.

Because government had played a principal role in Canada's economic development — underwriting the costs of canals, railroads, highways and airports; erecting protective tariffs and negotiating trade arrangements; using taxes, grants and subsidies to encourage some enterprises or restrain other economic activity; setting banking and securities policies; and creating dozens of Crown corporations to be producers of wealth and players in the so-called "mixed" economy — these new initiatives did not have to wait until a socialist or communist government came to power. An expanded role for government in Canadian economic enterprise came to be more or less mainstream. Liberal and Conservative governments, our country's seemingly non-socialist and highly pragmatic parties, continued to bridge any remaining gaps between the so-called public and private sectors to establish, in reality, Canada's single and functionally integrated *political sector.*

However, the sponge system in Canada does not merely entail a blending of public and private sectors for economic purposes. Rather, it is also the maturing and full-flowering of what has for decades been called our system of "brokerage" politics. Interests, demands and needs are brokered or traded for political support and votes in elections. Few have pretended seriously that our major parties are founded upon strong ideological differences; certainly for every item of ideology or philosophy that divides them, three others can be found that make them similar. The greatest distinction among our parties is whether they are in or out of office. The basic Canadian political ideology is pragmatism, which gave rise in the 1870s to "bridge and culvert" elections and in the 1990s to "infrastructure" elections. Same practice, rebranded.

We, as citizens, are likewise integrated into this system in a number of ways. First, Canadians who function in our sponge-like national community form our country's political class. Increasingly this class is not a traditional elite, as sociologists like John Porter chronicled in 1965 in *The Vertical Mosaic* or even more radical analysts like Wallace Clement portrayed in his 1975 treatise on *The Canadian Corporate Elite*, but has come to include *most Canadians*. We are less and less citizens who stand as separate human entities in relation to the Canadian state, and more and more like sponges ourselves in the way we relate to the daily practices and workings of the state and its many branches and programs. This does not mean that as citizens we run and control the state, but rather that because we are so controlled by its political processes, we have become transformed into creatures who must think and act politically at almost every turn in order to survive and function. We have each been co-opted — some to greater degrees than others to be sure — into this process.

Second, the artful dodges and cunning operations by which each one of us must every day deal with taxes, benefits, subsidies, constraining regulations, inspectors, forms, entitlements, illegalities and grant applications testify to our increased level of involvement. Our sphere of small "p" political action has become all-encompassing. The vast majority of Canadians are an integral part of this comprehensive sector of governance because new roles have been created by the interactive and mutually intrusive relationship between government and the social, cultural and economic organizations of Canada. There is widespread expectation within our political culture that government will — and ought to be! — party to any transaction or activity in the country, and this expectation has transformed the nature of our government's role and its relationship to us as citizens.

The third way in which citizens are absorbed by the Great Canadian Sponge is through our membership in organizations. When lobbyist Jack Slibar spoke to the researchers of the *underground royal commission*, he explained that "the vast majority of groups that work with government you never hear about and are so innocuous you would never even think they would do any kind of lobbying work." Slibar noted how Canadian society now has associations for all sorts of things. "If you look around this room," he said, "you see furniture, paintings, art, anything else along those lines, you could probably find an association that represents that particular sector. To a greater or lesser extent, they're going to have some formal or informal relationship with government." We each belong to organizations — whether for health, finances, environment, professional requirements, social issues or cultural activities — and have an expectation that they will be engaging government about matters on our behalf, and they do. In fact, it would be a challenge in Canada today to find an organization that does not lobby in one form or another, either through the activities of its own staff and members or by hiring a lobbying firm specializing in this work.

Because we live *inside* this all-encompassing reality, we accept the system and have become participants in it. It was not an explicit decision or conscious choice. Yet because the sponge-like nature of Canadian life is seldom acknowledged or accurately defined, we have remained perplexed when trying to figure out our own relationship with government. It's like we never got it, never caught on to the truth about what self-government really means.

Perhaps this lack of understanding is especially due to the fact that it is hard to reconnect citizens and government when the link of accountability has been severed between those who ask for benefits from government and the people who pay — which is to say, all of us who dwell in and constitute this Canadian Sponge. If, instead of getting money from the government in the form of an electronic deposit or a cheque in the mail, you had to meet with an individual taxpayer designated to make the payment directly to you, do you think that person or company representative would smile sweetly as he or she forked over the cash? The anonymity of the system changes behaviour because the sharp edge of reality is removed. In war, civilians on the ground might ask questions that the bomber pilot high overhead or the young missile launcher in a remote control room never get to hear. Similarly, in civilian society your designated taxpayer might pose a probing question or two that escapes the anesthetized attention of a civil servant whose own pay is directly deposited into a bank account and automatically rises when the cost of living increases. You yourself might even have second thoughts when hearing the response to your demand for money — "To do what?!" — if it was the face of another hard-working Canadian you saw, another taxpayer you held out your hand to, rather than a standard government application form. We are so myopic, soaked up inside our Great Sponge, that we seldom even recognize how much government has become a costly and all-embracing buffer in Canadian society.

This government role as buffer has also manifested itself in the blending of politics and industry that further characterizes the Canadian sponge system. Indeed, government and industry in Canada have long shared a symbiotic relationship. This relationship has been at the core of Canada's political sector, the blended realm of action in which government and business, supported by unions, community groups and special interests, participate in what has turned out to be an unaccountable partnership. Government thus became our fail-safe banker of last resort. Short-term political and economic pressures for decades pushed governments to supply funds and make other concessions to ill-fated businesses and dubious commercial ventures, and to sustain its own costly projects. Each case on its own may have been justifiable or at least politically plausible. The pressures are intense and many arguments rationalize putting more money in, such as "jobs, jobs, jobs" — the language that speaks to elected representatives. One by one, case by case, the reasons are always important, exceptional, justifiable. Over time, however, a cumulative pattern develops.

Free enterprise doctrine holds that risk takers win or lose and should be left free of government restraint in the marketplace to do just that: either reaping the rewards of success or paying the price of failure. Nevertheless, within Canada subsidies have reduced business risks by carrying them over into the Sponge, like an insurance program transferring to government the price for occasional failures. No businessman need take a full hit directly. The Sponge will absorb the blow. Corporations make their ultimate cash-call not to a company's shareholders and investors, but to taxpayers. Any Canadian who thought we just had an unemployment insurance program for workers but hadn't over the same half-century set in place a parallel program for companies and entrepreneurs who similarly lose their position "through no fault of their own" may be suffering from the myopia endemic inside the Sponge.

Subsidization is largely the same process as privatization, but in reverse. It becomes a vehicle for private enterprise at public expense, supported with little question and less scrutiny because our long-established public consensus or political culture says government should be a player in Canada's market economy. Understanding why it's fraudulently inaccurate to segment Canada into public and private sectors may help us to recognize the true nature of our Canadian Sponge, and thus begin to see more clearly how and why today's inexplicable problems seem so intractable.

When we speak of subsidization, many people think merely of the government paying out funds to some "private" companies and individuals, failing entirely to recognize that within the Great Sponge the flow is ubiquitous and two-directional: the subsidies *from* government are being paid for with subsidies *to* government. Consider, for example, the frequently contentious issue of the Government of Canada soaking up *billions* of extra dollars in payroll taxes from Canadian workers to ostensibly cover the needs of the unemployment insurance fund. This overtaking by government, far in excess of its needs for this fund, has been a hot political issue for a decade now. Nothing, however, changes. The reason is that the money is not just sitting in a pot — or even in an interest-bearing bank account — waiting to be spent when it's needed. It has gone into the Consolidated Revenue Fund and long since been spent. The "surplus" is a book entry; it exists only on paper. Because the government has a huge need for money, it pays current obligations, including subsidies, with whatever it can pool or scrape together. Many are deluded about this reality by the confusing names given to some of these programs, often in the Orwellian manner of Newspeak. Change the name and people may soon believe the reality itself has changed, especially as the new name is increasingly repeated. The Chrétien government, for example, changed the *Unemployment* Insurance Program to the *Employment* Insurance Program. Workers all the while are still heavily subsidizing government, in addition to all the regular taxes we pay.

This interpretation of the economies of the sponge sector is supported by a vast body of evidence, much of which is covered in more detail in other books reporting on the findings of the *underground royal commission*. Among these are *Taking or Making Wealth?* and *Guardians on Trial*, both edited by Anthony Hall and *Days of Reckoning*, edited by John Wood. Each elaborates on and substantiates, from contemporary Canadian experience, what is being discussed in an overview fashion here. In Canada's sponge system economic enterprises operate in a complex business culture that embraces government interaction and dependency ahead of risk taking and the play of market forces. Some business leaders still speak the private enterprise rhetoric of capitalism, even while they practise a form of corporate welfare in partnership with government. Over time the distinction between *government* ownership and control and *private* ownership and control has become virtually meaningless: at the functional level of the corporate entities, and at the behavioural level of the individuals who operate them, such a dichotomy no longer exists. This blending of the private and public sectors into a sponge has created a common Canadian culture that is averse to risk. Business ventures have been backed by government, and government speculation has been backed by taxpayers' resources, including corporate taxes and payroll taxes. The result is a Canadian version of a classic socialist state achieved in reverse: public ownership through private corporations, where our business leaders resemble functionaries and managers of state enterprises, certainly in practice if not in perception. How many government forms has your business filled out today?

The *underground royal commission* spoke with a manufacturer in southern Ontario, Colin Beasley, president of International Wall Coverings, who explained how government had encouraged the opening of a new wallpaper manufacturing company in a depressed economic region in Atlantic Canada using money taxed from existing Canadian wallpaper firms. The market was already perilous for existing manufacturers due to product oversupply, and most plants at the time were operating at only 65 percent capacity. Another wallpaper factory may have looked good to unemployed workers in the town with the new plant, but it seems perverse when looked at through the wider lens of accountability in government. What is more, the story does not end there. Beasley was asked directly if his firm got subsidies and he admitted it did, stating that "to not apply for funding that is equally available to any competitors would be irresponsible to the employees and shareholders of my company."

The fact is that subsidies are as Canadian as hockey. Right from the start of play our governments have provided extensive financial help through many different forms of subsidization, starting with the huge grants for the building of the Welland Canal between Lake Erie and Lake Ontario in the 1820s. Since then government has made payments or provided free land to citizens and companies. With the advent of regional economic development programs, it even subsidized entire regions of the country. The reasons given to justify the subsidies are varied: saving industries and jobs; creating employment; building up the physical and service facilities of the country; protecting the family farm; diversifying the economy of a province; or winning elections. Yet to assess the impact of these financial inducements, taken as a whole and considered for their cumulative effect over time, we need to ask this question: did the theory that government should prime the economic pump in order to start up a worthwhile industrial activity somehow become subverted into a practice whereby government didn't just help get the pump going, but ended up being responsible for its continuous flow too?

Once industry and politics were linked together in the Great Sponge, the stage was set for government to back losers rather than winners because of social and political pressures to respond to an immediate or urgently expressed need. For example, government subsidies have utterly transformed Canada's East Coast fishery, and not for the better. When Newfoundland had surplus labour in the 1960s and 1970s, Premier Joey Smallwood proposed that unemployment insurance be made available to fishermen in the winter if they had been fishing in the summer. At an earlier time in Canada a person who could not fish in winter would not have been considered "unemployed" and would have thought it ridiculous if you'd said he was. Seasonal work, like picking fruit or harvesting vegetables, was available *in season*. With the extension of unemployment insurance to seasonal workers, however, subsidies took on a whole new meaning, transforming unemployment insurance into a social entitlement.

Had the government even bothered to factor in the long-term economic implications of such a change before it decided to implement it? To find out, researchers for the *underground royal commission* decided to contact those who were working in Ottawa at the time. One who had paid close attention was Liberal MP Lloyd Francis, an economist who took seriously his role in the accountability process of responsible government. When Labour Minister Bryce Mackasey decided to extend unemployment insurance to seasonal workers in 1971, Francis met with the official who ran the Unemployment Insurance Commission, Clifford Murcheson. They felt the policy was wrong, recommended against it, warned it would destroy unemployment insurance. It would be a permanent subsidy to seasonal industry. It would keep too many people in seasonal employment who should shift to other areas with low unemployment. It would add enormously to the deficit of the UI Program. So Francis began raising questions, as he put it, "in the long-term interests of the country." The chairman of the parliamentary committee reviewing the amendments to the Unemployment Insurance Act told Francis he was "not being very helpful" and privately suggested he "get off the committee." He was in fact removed from the committee, and the government went ahead with the program expansion.

The result was that unemployment insurance became a massive subsidy program on the East Coast and the fishing industry became an employer of last resort. Anyone who couldn't get a job elsewhere could go to work in the fishing industry because in the winter he or she would automatically get unemployment insurance. The fishing industry became overloaded with people and pressure on the fish stocks mounted. Those trying to make a living by fishing earned very little income. Yet from where did even that income arise? Not from the fishery itself. "If you put together all the subsidies and payments made by the provincial government and the Government of Canada on the fishery, there were years in which the amount of money they spent was in excess of the value of the catch, and far in excess of the incomes earned by the fishermen," noted economist Parzival Copes, who spent many years studying the impact of government intervention on the fishing industry in Newfoundland. "Subsidizing an industry to more than 100 percent over an extended period is not sustainable, as time has shown in terms of the collapse of the fishery and the huge public debt that was amassed in the process."

The more intricately government became woven into the fishery, the more the industry became a blended area of activity in which no line could be identified between government or non-government responsibility. When the cod fishery closed down in 1991 because the fish were all gone, government paid off the workers. This dependency on government, which was now no different with or without the fish, caused those who felt they weren't getting enough money to occupy Government of Canada offices and demand more; the government caved in to the pressure and implemented another payoff program, The Atlantic Groundfish Strategy (TAGS). When TAGS ended they protested again. The program was extended. No fish were involved. Just sponge.

Thus the concept of accountability was transformed into a reverse doctrine of detrimental reliance ("Hey, government, we relied on you to our detriment! Pay us compensation!"). Since government was so involved and its participation had converted both the economic practices and cultural rhythms of the centuries' old fishing life into a government enterprise of vast and complex proportions, the people who were part of the industry had grown to expect support, then to depend upon it, and finally to demand it. Government had put the political dimensions of the fishery ahead of economic or environmental realities. Concluded Copes, "It's a misapplication of subsidies to pay them to industries that don't have a chance of making it in the long run." True accountability had diminished so much it just slipped through the net.

How government chooses which industries and businesses to back is an especially controversial topic because it is really government officials speculating with taxpayers' dollars. While some people look at such transactions with satisfaction (primarily those who benefit), others (usually those who must pay) view them with condemnation. Few remain neutral, however, because the costs and consequences of subsidization are far-reaching and ultimately touch us all.

Assessing the impact of subsidies is necessarily a complex matter. We find not only changes in economic activity itself (manufacturing, fishing, mining, farming, railroading) as direct and indirect consequences, but also the appearance of secondary and even tertiary activities that depend upon or result from the initially subsidized activity (for example, the banks, railroad and shipping companies and equipment manufacturers who all reap the economic spinoffs from farm subsidies). Proponents of subsidization might say, "Good, that's how it's supposed to work; it proves government was right to subsidize a lead industry if in turn it spawns more economic activity among its suppliers and customers." Others would hold their applause. For what we discover from the Canadian experience is that these additional ventures *also* cost tax dollars, that government has ended up subsidizing more or less entire sectors of the economy. In the words of Michael MacDonald, a one-time senior official with Ottawa's Atlantic Canada Opportunities Agency who was involved in directing subsidies and grants to Maritime businesses, "Ottawa is not in the economic development business. Ottawa is in the economic *dependency* business." The weak or nonexistent structures of accountability under which such programs operate, however, prevent the public from properly assessing them.

To get a better fix on whether, or to what extent, Canadians are reaping the benefits that ought to flow from an accountable system of government, we can consider policies in terms of broad links between economies and politics. As we've seen, one channel through which this economic-political-social connection gets expressed is that of subsidies, the payments that flow in all directions through, and are squeezed out of, our Canadian Sponge. In other cases, though, government runs the economic operation directly, through Crown corporations, public monopolies and other forms of public ownership, rather than disbursing funds to others. Just as subsidies can be thought of as private enterprise at public expense, as already mentioned, there is also the reverse phenomenon — public enterprise at private expense. Consider the example of public monopolies.

A public monopoly exists when the government blocks off an economic function and appropriates the running of it to itself, excluding by law any competitors. Utilities are a well-known example — from municipal franchises for electricity, water and waste management, to provincial hydro commissions, to the national Crown corporation for atomic energy. Inside our amorphous Sponge, we scarcely notice who runs or operates these things. Economics professor Gilles Paquet years ago posed the question, in our course on Canadian economic development at Carleton University in 1966, "Does a consumer really care who owns the power company, as long as when he flicks the wall switch the overhead light comes on?" For the most part, people only become interested in whether these are government monopolies when the status of ownership changes: when the private phone companies in Manitoba were bought up by the government to form a provincial telephone monopoly, for example; or when the private power companies were acquired by provincial power commissions in Ontario early in the 20th century to form Ontario Hydro; or when the Grand Trunk Railway and other bankrupt or teetering private railways were purchased by the federal government to form Canadian National Railway. By the same token, the sale of a government monopoly from time to time — such as liquor stores in Alberta, Hydro in Ontario or Air Canada nationally — also serves to remind Canadians that there are important structural features in our economy that are the consequence of government monopoly.

Yet in Canada our penchant to turn to government for support, not as a last resort but from the very first, is so ingrained in the country's functioning that it can be hard to see objectively the nature and extent to which public monopolies actually affect our lives. For much of the 20th century conventional wisdom in Canada held that nationalized, public sector companies should occupy a prominent place on our economic landscape, and that some areas of economic and commercial activity should be entirely the subject of government-controlled monopolies. Questions about accountability provide an overarching context in which to evaluate the performance of these monopolies. Moreover, there needs to be an objective standard, an independent set of criteria by which to measure whether these monopolies operate for the betterment or to the detriment of the country. At the very least, responsibility in government requires effective mechanisms of control and accountability so that performance can be held in check and related to the specific needs of the community as it evolves.

Whether they be in a monopoly position in the marketplace, as in the case of government-owned-and-operated utilities like telephones, electricity or railroads, or simply one of several players, as in the case of oil and rubber Crown corporations, the concept of government ownership has come under closer scrutiny in recent times. Deregulation and the partial sale of electrical power monopolies in provinces such as Alberta and Ontario make this an issue of personal concern to many Canadians. A society that can't boot up its computers, turn on its lights, turn up the heat in winter or air conditioning in summer, operate its factories, run its offices or schools, boil water or cook food is a society that pays attention. Like Alberta and Ontario, many governments have undertaken a program of privatization during the past dozen years, selling a number of publicly owned companies. What remains to be seen is whether privatization can re-establish the long-blurred line between the so-called public and private sectors of the economy. In Canada's experience one could say this is possible, but not probable. Some politicians and commentators have suggested that we have moved beyond an era in which players in (as they persist in describing it) our private sector would expect extensive grants, bailouts and subsidies to businesses. The evidence of this is inconclusive, as the Air Canada story — a saga in which a supposedly privatized company continually calls for government assistance — demonstrates.

In the context of this trend of increasing "privatization," which in a number of instances can only be accurately described as profit taking at the expense of taxpayers, many venerable institutions have come up for fresh-eyed appraisal. Government-owned monopolies, having over time become an established and accepted part of the Canadian political and economic landscape, pillars of our political sector, have faced increasing scrutiny and mounting pressures for change in order to cope with the powerful global economic pressures and new market conditions created by the various trade treaties into which Canada has entered.

Reasons that formerly drove governments into certain fields of economic activity — to support vulnerable or emerging enterprises — disappeared over time. Not only that, but the passage of time itself transformed the relationships between government monopolies and their clientele. For example, in 1935 the Government of Canada set up the Canadian Wheat Board as a Crown corporation to assist Western farmers in tackling the crises they were facing at the time: drought, deep economic depression and transportation challenges in bringing grain to market. For decades the Wheat Board seemed like the Rock of Gibraltar to Western farmers; it stood for stability when nothing else did. At the time of its creation, the board performed an important role in protecting farmers from the whims of elevator operators and speculators who were just as unaccountable then as parts of the Canadian Sponge have become today. However, what began as a fight for economic justice has now turned into anything but.

The Wheat Board is solely responsible for the sale of Western-grown grains within Canada and in export markets, either selling grains directly or through grain companies acting as its agents. The board also has extensive additional powers, including control over the amount of grain that farmers produce, delivery of grains into storage elevators, allocation of railcars to move grain and shipping of grain by seagoing freighters to foreign markets. Under the Wheat Board's marketing system, farmers deliver their grains to country elevators according to their quotas. From there the board arranges shipment to large terminals across the country. It pays farmers for their grain in two stages. The initial payment, set by Cabinet before the start of each crop year, provides farmers with a guaranteed minimum price when they deliver their grain. Handling costs at local grain elevators (over which farmers have no control) are, however, deducted before the board pays the guaranteed floor price to the farmer. If the Wheat Board is unable to recover this price through its sales in world grain markets, the shortfall is paid by the Canadian government. The second or final payment is made at the end of the year, and its size depends on the amount of money in the "pool" (if any) the board has left from selling the grain after paying all its salaries, commissions, benefits and administrative costs (over which, again, farmers have no control). Whether or not there is a final payment, and how large it is, must also be approved by Cabinet in Ottawa. From setting the price to backstopping the payments, there is no doubt that the Wheat Board is a hands-on government monopoly.

Western farmers might like or dislike the way the Wheat Board performs, but how do they really know what its performance ranking should be if there is nothing to compare it with? In a monopoly setting there really are no independent functional criteria by which to measure accountability objectively. You need a framework of standards and criteria for judging performance, and if there's no ability to compare, then there's really no basis on which to be held accountable. By definition a monopoly is the only show in town, so its operation has to be taken pretty much as it comes.

Many Prairie wheat farmers told the *underground royal commission* about the restraints they face in competing economically because of the bureaucratic controls and highly regulated production and marketing system for their grain. A rich body of evidence about the present-day issues surrounding the Wheat Board — including, ultimately, the concern for true accountability and fairness in finances and performance — is documented in the interviews featured in *Days of Reckoning*, edited by John Wood.

The central issue is whether the Wheat Board is still effectively performing its role as a public monopoly. Has it lost its original mission of helping Canadian wheat farmers when they cannot help themselves? A growing number of farmers have come to believe that it has become an out-of-date institution. Moreover, farmers aren't the only Canadians who have begun to question the role of government-owned monopolies in the economy. In the 1990s fierce debates arose across Canada questioning governmental practices that encourage the growth of monopolies, from the operation of public services and transit systems to the generation and sale of electrical power. Should monopolies even be part of Canadian industry? While much of the debate is framed in terms of security and safety or health standards, the deeper questions touch on both economic and political issues simultaneously through the common thread of accountability. Monopolies, insulated by their very nature from market forces, are themselves dangerously unaccountable sometimes, which increases the potential for inefficient economic practices. If costs don't matter, who cares?

In a self-governing country like Canada, in accordance with our ideology of democracy, we like to believe that government operates for the citizens, not the other way around. Yet of course we know that in practice it flows both ways. When the connection between the people and the government is financial, we see flow in one direction in such forms as taxes paid to support public programs and government operations, and also in rates paid for services and utilities; but the flow occurs in the other direction too, in terms of the government benefits paid out and public goods and services provided to citizens. However, as this chapter has also demonstrated, Canada's sponge system entails many more subtle and nuanced forms of integration than that. The artificial and conceptual boundaries between public and private, personal and political, industry and government do not exist. While the blending of these many realms means that citizens have become victims of an unaccountable government, the all-engulfing nature of the Sponge also means that we are implicated in the very causes of this problem.

9. Canadian Character in Its Contemporary Context

As individuals we are defined by the communities in which we live and derive our personal identity and purpose from the relationships we form in them. If we lived as isolated individuals, most everything we currently find ourselves doing would be pointless. Within community we divide up tasks so each of us can do what we are best at; working together through division and specialization of labour, we mutually serve each other's needs. Living in community implies dependence. Dependency is a natural state and interdependency the bond of a healthy community that has the ready capacity for self-control and accountability. Our sense of community is the lifeblood of the Canadian system of self-government.

However, the past decades, marked in part by the growth of government and also by changes in the expectations of Canadians, have witnessed the crossing of a subtle yet real threshold, from dependency into a new state of false dependency. That is, we have shifted from being a healthy and interactive community to one that is dependent on unsustainable programs and structures that do not reinforce our national self-reliance or our personal self-governance, or even our sustainability within the natural environment. This crossover marked the transition from a collective character of frugality, which had ensured financial accountability in the past, toward a culture of expectations and an indifferent acceptance of irresponsible government. The consequence is that when it comes to governing our country, on most matters we seem to be not only very busy, but also quite baffled.

An increasing false dependency both fuels and is supported by the growth of the so-called public sector, whose size soared through the 1960s and the 1970s. The range of administrative and benefits programs grew in scope, while government extended itself in new places and forms everywhere. Because this expansion was being played out on the solid stage of prosperous times, over the years of the long post-war economic boom, it seemed to be working. Or at least the problems that were being created by this new manner and style of governing were not, in such a context, readily apparent or willingly examined. Not everyone was blind to the problems inherent in the erection of a public infrastructure of false dependence. As William Mackness, financial expert and former Finance Department advisor, told researchers for the *underground royal commission*, "When these programs were being brought forward, I asked the obvious question. Why would you not do away with universality and save an immense amount of money?" The answer, a Liberal senator had confided to Mackness, was that "if you did that, you wouldn't maintain the support of the middle class for the expansion of the programs."

The result of this approach, buying off the voting middle classes by making them additional beneficiaries of programs thought to be aimed at alleviating poverty and improving the welfare of lower-income Canadians, had long-term consequences for the character of both the citizens and the country itself. "There is a very major commitment to universal social programs at all political levels in the country," observed Mackness. "If you don't think about it much, 'universality' has a nice ring. It is, however, very much an income-redistribution scheme that carries with it some quite untoward results, such as major subsidies from lower-income Canadians to middle- and upper-income Canadians."

When social security payments are made to all citizens regardless of need, as happens with universality, the result is a *total* welfare state. If social assistance went only to those who really needed it, much more could be done to reduce poverty without raising total social assistance costs. Yet instead of waging the hard political battle to extend benefits to those who really needed them, the way the CCF government of Tommy Douglas did in Saskatchewan in order to establish basic medical insurance, Ottawa opted for a more generous but less responsible course of giving benefits to all. Most parliamentarians who might have raised questions about the costs of this extravagant approach, which bought widespread electoral support even as it gave the back of the hand to the poor, did not. The few who did had so little leverage in the House of Commons, dominated by government ministers intent on carrying through their programs, that they might just as well have remained as silent as the rest. Nor did the government address such matters itself since it was not being forcibly required by Parliament to do so. How "responsible" had our government become by the 1960s? The erosion of accountability was well under way even more than three decades ago.

Paul McCrossan, a leading Canadian actuary who served several terms in office as a Tory MP from Scarborough, examined the record shortly after he arrived in the Commons and found that some half-dozen statutory benefits programs had been enacted by Parliament in the 1960s "with no cost estimates ever being made. The only open-ended social benefits program for which any projection of likely costs to the public treasury had been attempted was the Canada Pension Plan, and that estimate of future costs had been only for a decade." For all the rest, no sense of long-term financial implications, or even much question or debate, had engaged parliamentarians. The legislation for the MPs' own pension plan was passed in a single day, all three readings, so quickly not even a bill was printed in the routine parliamentary fashion. Such recklessness on the part of the government and inattentiveness on the part of Parliament was fuelled by a perception on the part of many Canadians that the country did not face serious financial problems. In summarizing the mindset of the time, McCrossan explained that many believed that "we could never have debt problems." People had become predisposed to not see any problem, which was not unreasonable in the circumstances. "Indeed," he continued, "we never did have any debt problems until the very late 1970s. We ran balanced budgets for 100 years."

It's hard to imagine now, but the euphoric mood in the 1960s and 1970s was unrestrained by the thought of money being limited. Economists teach about opportunity costs, but we heard the U.S.

president, Lyndon Johnson, tell his fellow Americans as they headed to war in Vietnam that tradeoffs would no longer be necessary, that the prosperous economy could afford "both guns and butter." Here in Canada, not surprisingly, the mood among those running our country was the same. "Money was a free good," said Allan Ross, whose career in Ottawa government financial circles, at Treasury Board and at the assistant deputy minister level, poised him well to observe the attitude toward financial responsibility of Canadian policy makers in the 1970s: "Only bean counters worried about money." This attitude created a deafness to any questioning voices.

Since virtually everybody was aboard Canada's extensive welfare state, total costs soared. These increases helped contribute to the creation of a national debt that would in time hobble us all and cause cutbacks in many of these self-same programs. Meanwhile, the gap between poor and wealthier Canadians remained substantively the same. Poverty is still with us today, despite our Canadian version of the welfare state, and in many cases, such as the increases in child poverty and homelessness, the situation is growing more, not less, desperate. Furthermore, in the years since the inception of these social programs most citizens developed new ideas about "entitlement" from government, a gradual yet real change in our character as a people. By being "everything to everybody" and not ever being held accountable for having taken the "soft" political choice, Canada's government and democratic process failed to create a stronger society free from poverty's scourge. How had Canadians come to see social benefits not as a generous provision of help in cases of special need, but instead something we are all entitled to as a right?

The *underground royal commission* posed this question to public administration professor Filip Palda. "Let me tell you about middle-class entitlements," replied Palda. "You're looking at one of the biggest beneficiaries of those entitlements — me!" The youthful academic explained how his education had been almost entirely paid for with public funds. He studied for a Ph.D. in the United States, paid for largely by the Canadian government. He pointed out how he takes the train each week, and that "half of that price is paid for because the train is subsidized." That's another few hundred dollars he picks up along the way. He noted that if he became unemployed, he'd get something like $735 a week for the length of his unemployment. "This is kind of strange because all these different kinds of programs were created to help the poor," he continued, "they were created to help people who are in trouble. The idea wasn't really to take the money away from the middle class and give it back to the middle class. When I sit back and ask myself what is going on here, I think that what is happening is that there's a separation in Canadian politics between people's actions and the consequences of those actions." What Palda described was erosion of accountability in its most basic sense.

While people gave over responsibility for their own family and neighbours, at the same time they knew they were also paying others, through their taxes, to shoulder these duties. We understood that in modern Canada government had social responsibilities well in hand because public agencies clearly had been mandated to address such problems — from hospitals to nursing homes to welfare offices to unemployment counselling services and safe houses for battered women and children. The nature of the social contract in Canada had been rewritten to include payment for a middleman: the professional social worker, government as our stand-in. We had evolved our very own made-in-Canada version of a social state.

Indeed, an increasing number of Canadians over the past couple of decades have held up Canada's social safety net as the very definition of our country, an example of Canadian values in operation. Ironically this is all too true. Have these programs served their intended purpose? Did the specific measures chosen (a baby bonus cheque for every mother, unemployment insurance for seasonal workers) successfully implement the values of care and compassion which lay behind them? If lower-income Canadians subsidize higher-income Canadians in a range of areas from education to health care, is that because we are uncharitable to those in need, or incompetent at designing programs that actually help those requiring assistance beyond their own ability to pay? In the decade since the Government of Canada co-chaired a United Nations initiative for the world's children and we "declared war" — in Prime Minister Brian Mulroney's words — "on child poverty," the number of Canadian children living below the poverty line, as previously noted, has risen from one in seven to one in five (as of May 2002). This is the reality, and the questions which arise from it bring us back squarely to accountability.

Our government has become like a shrouding veil that separates us as individuals, as neighbours, as communities. Canada has ended up as an amorphous entity of all sorts of groups, quietly extracting money through government from each other, right and left, with middle-class groups and business corporations having the greatest power to draw from this fluid flow of funds. By the early 1970s, in fact, a great many businesses were benefiting from grants and subsidies. Wealthier people who owned and ran companies received their social and business benefits yet complained about "welfare bums" in society. So much for the plan of keeping the opinion leaders "on side" by paying them off with benefits under universal programs! David Lewis, national leader of the New Democratic Party at the time, in a speech at New Glasgow, Nova Scotia, on August 3, 1972, responded in defence of low-income beneficiaries by observing that the country was filled with "*corporate* welfare bums."[10] He made a telling point. It seemed inappropriate to be chastising the poor for receiving welfare when just about everybody else in the country was on some benefit program, subsidy or corporate dole from government. Even more perverse was the fact that, as these benefits became entrenched in people's expectations, efforts to be accountable and correct the untoward results of social and health programs were resisted. Middle-class entitlements continued to be subsidized by low-income people; government funding continued to keep uneconomic or poorly managed businesses afloat; and the complex interworking of various statutory regimes to provide social assistance kept the working poor in a poverty trap by penalizing their modest gains.

Canada's early social reformers waged long and acrimonious battles to get better programs — pensions, health care, affordable housing — for poor and low-income Canadians. Theirs was not a campaign to help people who were already managing quite well on their own, but a quest for social justice. An absence of accountability, however, translated their noble ideas about being our brother's and sister's keeper into a welfare state in which benefits were not concentrated on those in need. Today unemployment insurance is commonly given to people whose income exceeds the national average. Film production subsidies are given to wealthy producers and production houses. Hospitals, while funded by revenues collected from Canadians at every income level, have been found to provide better service to upper- and middle-income patients who, because of social contacts, engage in "queue jumping." How did we fool ourselves into thinking we have a welfare state based on compassionate help for people who really need it? In truth we are all just grabbing for ourselves benefits and services that most of us could afford, or could afford to do without. If asked, many Canadians would justify our appetite for benefits by saying that we've been made to pay for them and this is the only way in the present system to recover our losses. They would exhibit less a sense of guilt than an assertive attitude of entitlement.

Government may be carried out through institutions, but institutions do not operate without people. We interact with our democratic institutions daily. Winston Churchill observed, "We shape our institutions, and then they shape us." Both our intrinsic human character and our particular attributes as Canadians are moulded by the circumstances (social, cultural, economic and political) in which we find ourselves. Yet we are scarcely passive in the process. We also exert through our expectations and behaviours an influence over our surroundings and circumstances.

This inquiry into accountability has shown there have been significant changes in Canadian character, changes by definition highly relevant to our process of self-government. During his discussions with the *underground royal commission* Gordon Robertson touched upon something invisible that had previously held government spending in check: a Canadian sense of frugality. When government started growing exponentially, Robertson said, he was "surprised at the proliferation of government programs, about the very great growth in government apart from social security." He pointed to "subventions for all sorts of lobby groups of different kinds, that sort of thing. These did surprise me, concern me a bit that we were going too far." Once prudent penny-pinching had prevailed in Canadian society and by extension within government. When this attribute disappeared, an unseen restraint on spending also retreated into the recesses of history. With it would soon go Canada's world-renowned reputation for sound public finance. Not all tripwires are physical or procedural; some of the most effective reside within instinct and are embodied, or can be, in character.

The tumultuous struggles in recent years to control spending have largely been efforts to institutionalize procedures, set up rules, establish better government watchdogs — all to substitute for that infallible tripwire of the old system: a frugal approach to the public purse. Yet financial restraint wasn't the only control that disappeared; more profoundly, the underlying set of values that created such restraint had also left us. Values by their very nature cannot be "seen," and unlike more tangible manifestations of government such as the Supreme Court buildings or the National Research Council laboratories, they are carried largely inside us as individuals. When members of Canada's public service from the older generation retired, they were replaced by a younger, post-Depression, post-war generation. The values held by this new crop of civil servants were so different from those of their predecessors that the Canada of the 1970s, 1980s and 1990s seemed like a foreign country to any who had travelled through these same parts in the 1950s.

Historian Donald Creighton, himself a Canadian of this earlier vintage, suggested that all history is the outcome of "character and circumstance."[11] Circumstances we can see and measure — volume of trade, shortage of water, number of jobs, level of income, size of national debt, burden of taxation, riots, famines and wars. Most of what Creighton calls "circumstance" we can quantify or describe as fact because it appears in tangible, physical form. Yet how do you see values or measure character?

Character is as character does. It forms the foundation of government's approach to public affairs and acts as the basis for political decision making. When we examine the character of the members of that older generation, three attributes in particular stand out. First, they had an almost visceral sense of urgency about being their brother's keeper. This resolve was bred into their bones by the human sheltering and mutual support needed to survive the Depression and then endure the Second World War. If the strongest steel comes from the hottest part of the furnace, these Canadians, neither raised in comfort nor flabby in their thinking, had been resolutely strengthened in their public purposes. They were clear about what mattered, and while extremely world-minded and living life robustly, they were seldom self-indulgent. The second attribute was their frugality. In their personal lives they lived by a code of saving, prudently setting aside money against the rainy day that experience had taught them would inevitably arrive. They always knew there would be a day of reckoning. Third, they were self-reliant. These Canadians had, in many adventuresome ways, learned to fend for themselves. Their belief about saving enough money to buy something rather than purchasing it on credit expressed an instinctive fear of becoming beholden to someone else.

This generation's idea of creating a welfare state was not born of an abstract political ideology any more than it sprang from some perverse thought of making everyone dependent upon government. Rather, it came directly from searing experiences of the Depression and a steely resolve to ensure no one in dire circumstances would suffer that way again. The goal was a better division of the nation's resources for the people of the nation through a system of economic and social justice. The idea was to create opportunity and provide encouragement for people to retain or regain self-sufficiency. Those who pioneered many of these programs were frugal people looking for fairness to all. I believe they would recoil at the thought of creating generations of people dependent upon government. They might also be shocked to discover how the pressure of special-interest groups turned Canada into a welfare state that benefits the middle class and business corporations rather than those who warrant social or economic support from government. They might angrily rebel against our massive public debt, which has crushed the life out of so much of what they painstakingly coaxed into existence.

One by one these older guardians passed through their retirement parties, out of the public service and into the pasture of policy institutes and pensions. With them departed values that had helped make and keep Canada the true north, strong and free. From their retirement perches these elders observed what was flowing in behind them, as the underpinnings of the old order washed away. It took about two decades for this collapse to become complete, to become recognizable for what it truly was. Without the restraints their values had created, what could hold spending in check? The entire operation of Canadian government did not hinge upon these values alone; there were also administrative procedures and institutional arrangements to maintain the order of responsible government. Yet, as noted, even many of these — from the Office of the Comptroller General to the annual approval of the Estimates by Parliament — had been eroded so greatly as to be as good as abandoned. It was not a coincidence that these mechanisms for accountable and responsible financial control disappeared at the same time the older values of frugality were being eclipsed. It was partly a change in procedures and institutional practices, but it was also a transition point in an important aspect of Canadian character.

Some Canadians still faithfully describe our government as one of our national assets. With patriotic devotion some still just automatically salute the forms and symbols of our governing structures, but refuse to acknowledge the rhythmic functions of government operations behind them. A child seldom wants to hear about or even acknowledge the sex life of his or her parents. Perhaps only in this respect, many Canadians currently act like the shy children of our government. When we are so bound to government, we are the same as government. Those who recoil from such a thought would be equally dismayed to discover that, as Sean Moore in Ottawa put it, "We have seen the enemy, and it is us." In Canada's government-dominant system, with our highly evolved and seamlessly integrated sponge-like political sector, "they" have indeed become "us." This symbiosis means that we share responsibility for successes and failures. If government is unaccountable, we don't need to hold up a magnifying glass to see why. A mirror will serve just as well.

Our system today is so integrated that we cannot distance ourselves enough to separate function from form, to provide arm's length evaluation in making strategic decisions about the allocation of resources. This is why and how we have imperceptibly but steadily converted self-government to self-interest government. If there were more objectivity, there could be greater accountability. Our political institutions, created to provide for a rule of law and public-interest outcomes, have been so undermined as to have now left us in the void, suffering an absence of accountability. Accountability is not some theoretical problem, but a pragmatic and costly reality. Canadians are inventive and highly practical; if we begin asking fresh questions, it could prompt better answers about why we have been so accepting of waste and failure. We should capitalize on our knowledge and experience for the benefit of our country, just as we would do for ourselves. It is a matter of character.

A nation has both physical and moral assets. The only way they can be combined, however, is through the people of the country. A citizen may have duties to vote and pay taxes and obligations to live under the rule of law and in harmony with the rights of others, but beyond this a citizen has the higher calling of character. What does character in citizenship really mean? I believe that in a self-governing country essentially it means "to thine own self be true."

Once citizens might have insisted that it was not merely social programs that defined Canada as a nation. They would have proudly spoken of and told stories that showed how enterprise, adventure and self-reliance defined both this country and our people. Am I writing here with a bit of hubris or a sense of nostalgia? I don't believe so. A sense of community can be grander and more uplifting than the universe of generally applicable social programs. Today social justice in our country certainly includes governmental programs and civil administration, but only a dispirited and timid character would hold that the essence of Canadianism is restricted to or confined by them. Somehow we have come to embrace minimum standards as our Canadian common denominator, implying that we are capable of agreeing upon no higher cause or greater national purpose.

Responsible government was once such a reflection of our collective character, and the very signature of our individual characters. We, as Canadians, *were* responsible government. In self-governance we had sought balance between individual freedom on one hand, and community sharing on the other, all within a sovereign country. Yet this vision of our society — the Canada of throbbing promise, a modern state embracing responsible government and healthy security for its diversely enterprising citizens — during the past 30 years became more like some point on a receding horizon. For self-government would surely entail accountability, and that, in its most profound sense, had vanished. The evolution of our collective character was inextricably linked to the erosion of accountability, the slipping away of a Canadian possibility of self-government.

This loss of sovereignty within our own country only made it harder to withstand assaults on our national sovereignty from without, as we see now only too painfully, on a vast scale and in telling detail, day by day. The reasons we are vulnerable as a nation have less to do with the strength or agendas of foreign interests than with the weakness of our own governing character, including a shortsighted unwillingness to be accountable. We now turn to how citizens' attitudes and behaviours, not as they once were but as they are today, have evolved to deal with this transition through the development of escape mechanisms.

10. Escape Mechanisms

Citizen Alternatives to Dysfunctional Government

If a citizen believes government is wasteful, confusing and inexplicable, he or she may actively protest or just passively lose interest. The latter is why we have seen voter participation in elections steadily declining. We're pretty familiar with the formal expressions of protest, the kind that take on a political, procedural or institutional nature, the sort that can be dramatic enough to capture the attention of television news cameras and the interest of political parties. So what we'll focus on here, instead, are the less visible responses. Some of these are invisible because nobody who's making a stealthy getaway wants to draw attention to himself or herself.

Protest by escapism does say a lot about the nature of our Canadian "character and circumstance." Behaviourists note that when we are faced with a threat, instinct guides us to either fight or flee, depending on which alternative is probably best for survival. In our political life we are witnesses to both battles and retreats, a collective expression of this same phenomenon. Culturally, a lot of what we do may seem like escapism, a way of coping with sordid reality by taking a mental trip elsewhere. The general nature of North American culture involves escapism on a grand scale, a holiday from history. Given the frustrations that a Canadian citizen experiences because our government is confusing, wasteful and inexplicable, why should we be surprised if individuals seek an outlet to preserve sanity, perhaps even to enhance their well-being? The circumstance in which we find ourselves is that of living under a largely dysfunctional system of government. Citizens find escape hatches to deal with the lack of accountability in the system. In most cases it's not because we have all the information about what's wrong. How could we, since government is so artful at concealing much of it and "spinning" what does come out? Nor are escape routes being taken, in most cases, because citizens have given deep reflection to these matters or analyzed them in terms of responsible government or the decline of accountability. Most of us arrived where we are now simply by coping in our own lives with the consequences of the unresponsive and irresponsible nature of many aspects of Canadian government.

Just consider the volatile topic of taxes. When a citizen believes that government is wasteful, he or she will resent paying hard-earned money in taxes, which is why in the 1980s we saw the beginning of a tax revolt that continues to this day. There's often more involved than meets the eye, however. There is a link, as we'll see in this chapter, between these taxation issues and the erosion of accountability. It is not just that people are disgruntled because they have to pay taxes or that the tax laws are confusing. It is that the accountability process that would allow people to know where their money is going to be sent.

The tax bond is one of the strongest connections between citizen and state. Under our system of responsible government, one of Parliament's most important functions is to "control the public purse strings," to oversee the collection of public funds (by passing tax legislation) and to make sure that, once collected, taxpayers' money is used wisely (by approving the Estimates). Parliament, in theory at least, was to have been our institutional forum for accountability. It is in this relationship that citizen and government each makes its strongest claims on the other: the government for money, the citizen for accountability in its use. The political emotion invested in this relationship is easily detected when someone stops talking in disengaged terms about "public revenues" and starts to viscerally refer instead to "my tax dollars!"

The Income Tax Act of Canada inculcates a sense of duty with respect to taxation. It was founded on the honour system, based on the premise that citizens will declare their full income and pay the stipulated level of tax. Once this code of civil understanding wears thin, however, the tax collector proves to have an iron fist inside the velvet glove of voluntary compliance. Workers who have had their wages garnished by the Canada Customs and Revenue Agency understand the power of the state to collect money it claims is owing. Property owners who cannot pay municipal taxes and watch their properties disappear in a tax sale know about this power too. Small businesses, struggling to provide payroll cheques and fulfill a role in the local economy, have likewise learned how unrelenting the state can be in demanding its due, for "rendering unto Caesar what is Caesar's."

At the end of the day many Canadians question the fairness of the tax system. Specialists who conduct in-depth studies of taxation's impact document specifically how unfair it really is and how the promise of "progressive taxation" is not at all delivered in operation. In Canada this primary relationship between citizen and state has deteriorated for a number of reasons: the complexity of taxation; the hassles of the multidimensional collection system with its variety of different tax collectors from the national, provincial and local governments; the perception and the reality of wasted public money; and clear evidence of a double standard that benefits the rich and powerful. To these resentments, of course, we can also add both the sting of having to hand money over and the prevailing sense that tax levels are too high. Canadians' feelings about taxation have grown sharper in response to a pattern of waste and unaccountability in government spending. By the 1980s a number of taxpayer organizations had sprung up and in general Canadians felt less inclined to pay taxes. An added sense of futility, even despair, arose as taxpayers realized that some $40 billion in Canadian tax revenue was being consumed each year just to pay interest on the national debt, and that about half of that money was being paid to lenders outside the country, a further huge drain on our economy.

One way people can fight the system is through a tax revolt, using public protest to agitate for changes in the tax system. In extreme cases protesters take actions to change the system of government itself, actions which may reach the level of a revolution. Another way to opt out is to leave the country, or at least to ship one's money offshore. People who can expeditiously remove themselves from a jurisdiction they feel is taxing them to death do so. As tax historian Charles Adams told the *underground royal commission*, "Patriotism is soluble in taxes." These individuals tend to share two attributes: their high income attracts large tax bites that fuel their resentment toward government, and they are, because of their wealth and social position, quite mobile, certainly more so than average wage earners. So they relocate to the tax havens of the world: Luxembourg, Jersey, Ireland, Cyprus, Cook Islands, Barbados, or any of the other places that our bright young tax experts and financial advisors are able to point to from their polished office towers in our major cities. Books and guides are published in Canada to assist this form of escape.

It's not only the well-off who choose to relocate. This trend is also increasing among enterprising young Canadians. Beyond their understandable resentment and resolve to turn away, which is a further cost of this large pattern of unaccountable and costly government, youth's close connection with innovation and technology presents new possibilities. For if their interest cannot be kept here in Canada, there are better choices south of the border. Canadians looking for opportunities have long been voting with their feet: moving out of Canada to the United States. A lot of our best and brightest have taken off. The number of highly trained young people who each year leave Canada to work in the United States is equivalent to the output of two and a half Simon Fraser Universities. How are Canada's interests being served running two and a half universities for the United States? Vancouver-born Chris Taylor, who owns a video-game design company near Seattle, had a choice whether to start his business in Canada or the U.S. "Canada, with all the taxes and with the dollar, unfortunately is very weak and it just doesn't make sense, you know? Why would a person start something and automatically penalize themselves right out of the starting gate. A tax structure like that chases money away. It's like, governments don't think this will happen?"

The U.S., meanwhile, facilitates the flow, while its policy framework makes the economic choices easy. American companies and business schools purposely cream the Canadian crop and as a result get "the brains" that are the best of our best. Most of those who escape to the U.S. by their very natures are generators of employment. "If your entrepreneurs in Canada continue to migrate south, then Canada's going to be the poorer," explained David Blumberg, a venture capitalist who lived in Canada for many years but now resides in San Francisco. "If a few percent leave and they are the entrepreneurial percent or they are the scientific elite, or they are the entertainment elite, or they are the athletic elite, or they're the best lawyers or the best doctors, what's going to happen to the rest of society? The rest of society is going to be poorer for it."[12]

Citizens unhappy with their tax situations can respond by leaving the country or putting their money offshore into tax havens; another method of escape is to keep the money here and just leave off paying the country's taxes. Indeed, many citizens have simply been opting out of Canada's tax system by participating in the underground economy. In other words, people choose to no longer play by the official rules and, consequently, pay over less of their money in taxes. They ignore the regulations outlined in the great book of taxation sport, the Income Tax Act, and move instead into a different arena. They conduct their economic transactions partly through a system of barter, partly through the code of silence between co-conspirators. Cheques are replaced by cash, invoices by oral agreements, advertisements by word-of-mouth references.

During the 1980s in Canada it probably became archaic to speak any longer of an "underground" or "black market" economy. A more accurate term would be the "parallel" economy, one which has come to function more and more openly as time has gone by. The rise of this parallel economy is hardly surprising, considering that most Canadians find our government and its tax laws confusing. Once we had an adage that "a citizen should understand the law by which he or she is taxed." This idea, so fundamental to good government, was long ago lost in the deep complexity of Canada's tax system — which is why numerous businesses have sprung up to prepare other people's income tax returns for them. Citizens who really don't understand the tax laws feel estranged from the system and have diminishing respect for it. The drive for tax simplification, even for a "flat-rate tax," has its origins here. The complexity of the tax system is beyond comprehension for most of us. Yet even if we cannot truly understand all the ways in which the system works, we understand fully its implications — because the system still gets our money. We thus have both a visceral and financial awareness of its reality. That is why taxes, when linked with concern about government spending, raise the truly serious challenge for a citizen who begins to ask the hard and simple question, "What is *really* happening in there with my money?"

This question is an important first step toward consciousness of accountability. Once asked, the next step along the route of inquiry is crucial because it requires us to make a choice. Along one path we are pushed into a state of mind where it seems rational to believe it's time to opt out. In the other direction we push harder to get reform, change, accountability. The former is a sort of revenge, the latter a kind of responsibility.

The tax system, as noted, is the most important connection between people and government. Charles Adams said it is like the covenant exchanged in a marriage vow. If there is a single test by which to validate the sanctity of this bond, it is accountability. The vow covers "for better and for worse," Adams reminded us, "it does not cover infidelity." When government squanders money it abuses the trust and violates the pact. That is why a tax revolt is about much more than just money. It is about fairness and fidelity, sought by citizens who see that they no longer get it — in the form of accountability — from their government. Between citizens and government, tax is the earnest money of a basic understanding of the fundamentals, and this agreement, which is both implicit in our actions and explicit in our laws and institutions, is sometimes called the "social contract." A social contract involves an exchange, and the core bargain is money given in taxes in exchange for accountability in spending. If "no taxation without representation" was once the rallying cry, "no representation without accountability" would be the appropriate successor axiom for today.

Our tax collection system still works; government revenues continue to flow in. Yet a significant number of citizens has chosen to opt out of the tax regime, and once this step has been taken it is not easy to go back. Like a good marriage, good governance is based on mutual respect. When such opting out occurs in an organized and self-governing society, citizens and government become estranged from one another. Government loses more than just money. As citizens increasingly see government as something they have come to resent, this loss of respect jeopardizes democratic government of the kind we once endeavoured to operate in Canada.

Analysis and public criticism show serious flaws with the tax system and the way it is implemented. What larger mechanism, if any, exists within our self-governing society to bring about a course correction? We already see that we can no longer look to Parliament to call the government to account. So who can we hold accountable?

Where We Are Going

11. Our Quest to Regain Responsible Self-Government

At this point you might be feeling so discouraged that it seems a good idea just to lie back and let the U.S. finish taking over. If we've grown so ineffective in managing our affairs because our governing system is profoundly dysfunctional, why struggle any longer? Is resistance really futile? When we feel ill and lethargic for a troublingly long time, when we don't know what's wrong with us, just that something clearly is, that our energy is drained and our spirit is sapped by uncertainty, the best thing to come along — even before a cure — is a good diagnosis.

This book certainly is not intended to encourage us to give up our Canadian passports or flee to another country. The intent, instead, is to contemplate what *Canadian citizenship*, perhaps for the first time in our history, could truly mean.

Given the current condition of Canada as an integrated political-economic sponge, we are living neither outside nor inside a culture that embraces accountability; we do not have the arm's length relationships, the constitutional jurisdictions, the parliamentary processes, nor even the political analysis that allows us to be held to account, except in some lingering technical senses of the word. It's important to know that because history has shown accountability to be a key factor in the survival of human societies. Accountability is a bigger concept than accounting or allocating blame or even responsible government itself. It is the handmaiden of success. Without accountability a system becomes dysfunctional over time. That's another way of saying it does not work well, and the longer you operate an apparatus that cannot do what it is supposed to or what you expect it will, the worse things get. You yourself end up getting screwed by your own government.

In these pages we've been looking back for accountability, but only because of our need to move forward with success. The purpose of a rear-view mirror isn't to provide nostalgia about where we've been but to safely position ourselves in heavy traffic and see what's roaring up on us from behind. The grand, aggregated, *total result* of government operating in the way it now does in Canada is an overwhelming sense of confusion. Confusion is worse than frustration or anger because it actually *prevents* response. Feelings of frustration or anger can become engines for action; but when we're confused we cannot distinguish between purpose and performance, or between policy and procedure, and thus cannot grasp the relationship between cause and effect either. As Canadian government keeps going in circles, we get even more confused; and the more confused we become, the more confusing it all gets. Because we no longer even understand the system, we make contradictory demands upon it and have uncertain expectations of it. More than a dizzying merry-go-round, it has now become a vicious cycle.

In order to get as clear and dispassionate a view of our present circumstances as subjective humans can, and in order to understand why government in Canada has become wasteful, incomprehensible and unaccountable, we need to rethink our history and its presumptions. If it weren't for our country's many good points and redeeming features, this picture of how we've allowed our system of government to institutionalize failure ought to leave us feeling fully depressed. Even the simple exercise of juxtaposing Canadian strengths and national assets beside the real nature of Canadian government is not easy: our minds tend to blur the two as one. The Canadian Sponge is all-embracing. We are so utterly living inside the structures and practices of our Sponge — what in some other countries might be called instead "the State" — that we do not see beyond it, cannot see ourselves operating outside the confining security of its many compartments and interstices. We see our government and ourselves as integrated. "If we can't get a grant for this," I've heard it said adamantly both in and out of public life, "it won't be done!"

This book tells a tale that may appear at first to be about politics, but it is really the story of our political culture, and cultural life is measured neither by time nor money but by experience and the character of people. This book presents as sincerely as possible the real experience of actual Canadians. It provides a new portrait of our country that has neither a private nor a public sector but a space in between; not a no man's land but rather everyone's land, occupied by most Canadians, noble sponges or statists all. The term "sponge" is not used to be derisive, but in the hope of freshly conveying a better understanding of what we have become, a different insight into who we are.

Those at the apex of Ottawa's institutions of power, the civil service mandarins, and those in the party political class who interact effectively with them all defend the system's credibility. They do so in many forms and fashions. Yet following years of growing discomfort in Ottawa, where I saw the dysfunction and malfunction of this very system in even the most elemental matters, I set about, after leaving Parliament, to test their claims. Defenders of the Canadian status quo, whether for reasons of privilege or inertia, or both, have been stonily unreceptive to a new partnership between the Canadian people and government. Always they have *rested their defence on a claim of competence and credibility*. It cannot be denied that those who speak for the Government of Canada command apparent legitimacy. They have the advantage of power and prestige of office, both of which are handy when it comes to shucking off others who assert that the system they control is neither competent nor credible. Yet our best civil servants know better than anyone how much waste and inefficiency government contains. In the prevailing culture of the past three decades, though, they have had little real incentive, and considerable disincentive, to push very hard to correct such problems, or even to draw them seriously to public attention.

Accountability is an ethical quest and social imperative before it is a political doctrine. It is a permanent reminder of the perils of political life and potentials of public affairs. Accountability teaches us the vigilance we require, if not to achieve some receding utopia, then to at least avoid the approaching dystopia — the world in which the worst things we fear become our realities. Canadians deserve to understand why our institutions of government seldom function the way we are told they do. When someone says, "You really don't want to know!" we probably need to. Canadians are also entitled to express doubt when we witness how stated policies and announced programs do not lead to the goals originally proclaimed. Why, for instance, after 30 years of programs designed to eliminate regional economic disparity in Atlantic Canada, does this region still have the same wage gap and poverty levels it had, relative to the rest of the country, before the multibillion-dollar programs began? Why did areas of Western Canada long primed for the development of secondary manufacturing and service industries hit major disincentives in bringing these industries into being? Why should poverty and homelessness and illiteracy in Canada be so dramatic following years of an operating welfare state? Turning to the future, what are the attitudes and outlooks of younger Canadians, the new generation that is inheriting this dysfunctional system of government and the yet-to-erupt implications of the huge national debt left behind for it?

These questions, and the issues that attend them, require a response. Indeed, some of what is currently on our country's public agenda entails efforts to address such problems. This discussion will not end, however, with a checklist of proposed reforms, for the purpose of this book is not to present the policy platform of a political party or to outline a program developed by of one of our country's policy think tanks. These pages are instead an invitation to reflection, an exhortation to ponder, a little more deeply, our Canadian condition and the place and purpose of each of us who are citizens of this country. History's successful reformers, as suggested in an earlier chapter, have always been the ones who first came to a profound understanding of the true nature of the problems their societies confronted, not the ones who quickly rushed to push through a series of solutions. Sometimes the greatest reforms of all can be quite simple to implement because they are so basic. At this juncture in Canada's evolution I believe what we need most to see and understand clearly, what can carry us to a more harmonious and fulfilling future, is less heat and more light — light that will provide insight into the issues that surround us.

If there is to be a contemporary re-expression of national purpose through forms of responsible government, whether by political and institutional change, or by means of a cultural re-confederation, it will come increasingly through the new approaches of younger Canadians. Too many in middle age are the overweight beneficiaries of a bloated system they themselves have enjoyed and have no incentive to change. The public order to which younger Canadians must respond is vastly different from the one their predecessors encountered in the 1960s and 1970s. The outlook of today's youth is in many respects more realistic, more self-reliant and even idealistic, in a more focused and personal sense of that word, than the national or global idealism of earlier generations. I see this not just in the university lecture hall with hundreds of students at a time, but in countless conversations we share one on one. I observe it, too, in many places off campus and across most parts of our country. If Canada can link the newly synthesized culture of this rising generation with the operation of an altered structure for more accountable government, we still have a shot at becoming winners in the 21st century. We may yet find a way to outpace and distance ourselves from the four horsemen of Canada's apocalypse.

Being accountable, after all, does not require us to come up with some form of moralistic redress for past errors or present omissions; it does require coming to terms with what has really happened and knowing why, and so understanding where to go from here. Making that link, with all the controversy, realism and wit that it entails, can yet render things explicable and can form the true basis for regaining responsible self-government.

Our character as Canadians is what emerges from all this. These days many people question the absence of ethical conduct in government. This apparent turmoil in ethics, however, is not inexplicable, considering the present state of our collective Canadian character. The word "ethics," after all, comes from the Greek word meaning "character." As Kitson Vincent kept repeating, like a mantra, in the trenches and command posts of the *underground royal commission*, "Character is as character does." Self-government is in our own hands. If each of us accepts that accountability entails nothing more — but certainly nothing less — than being responsible to that truth, we may yet realize our greatest potential as Canadians. As we think, so shall we act.

Notes

1. Richard Phidd, *The Leadership Challenge: Effectiveness in the 21st Century* (Guelph, Ontario: University of Guelph, 2002) p. 10.
2. David Beatty, *Constitutional Law in Theory and Practice* (Toronto: University of Toronto Press, 1995) p. 47.
3. FLQ: Front de Libération de Québec.
4. For a thorough account of Couchman's experiences, see *Reflections on Canadian Character: From Monarch Park to Monarch Mountain* by Bob Couchman.
5. Richard Gwyn, *The Northern Magus* (Toronto: McClelland & Stewart, 1980) p. 365.
6. Robert Sheppard and Michael Valpy, *The National Deal: The Fight for a Canadian Constitution* (Toronto: Fleet Books, 1982) pp. 22–23.
7. Sheppard and Valpy, p. 23.
8. Sheppard and Valpy, p. 23.
9. Michael Adams, *Environics Election Report 1988*, No. 3 (Toronto: Environics Research Group, 1988), p. 4.

10. See David Lewis, *Louder Voices: The Corporate Welfare Bums* (Toronto: James Lewis & Samuel, 1972).

11. Donald Creighton, in an interview with Allan Anderson, *Graduate*, University of Toronto, June 1968.

12. For more information on the "brain drain," see *Goodbye Canada?* by Paul Kemp.

Index